FREE TRADE AGREEMENTS AND OTHER CONSULTATIONS UNDER TRADE PROMOTION AUTHORITY

FREE TRADE AGREEMENTS AND OTHER CONSULTATIONS UNDER TRADE PROMOTION AUTHORITY

GOVERNMENT ACCOUNTABILITY OFFICE

Nova Science Publishers, Inc.
New York

For permission to use material from this book please contact us:
Telephone 631-231-7269; Fax 631-231-8175
Web Site: http://www.novapublishers.com

Library of Congress Cataloging-in-Publication Data

Free trade agreements and other consultations under trade promotion authority / Government Accountability Office.
p. cm.
ISBN 978-1-60456-393-1 (hbk.)
1. Free trade--United States. 2. Commercial treaties--United States. I. United States. Government Accountability Office.
HF1756.F726 2008
382'.973--dc22 2008000026

Published by Nova Science Publishers, Inc. ✦ New York

CONTENTS

PREFACE

This book reviews what FTAs have been pursued under TPA and why Overall, what is the economic significance of these agreements to the United States? What is the nature of the consultation process for Congress and how well has it worked in practice? What is the nature of the consultation process for private sector trade advisory committees and other stakeholders, and how well has it worked in practice?

WHY GAO DID THIS STUDY

Congress granted the President Trade Promotion Authority (TPA) to negotiate agreements, including free trade agreements (FTA) in 2002. TPA stipulated negotiating objectives and procedural steps for the administration, including consulting with Congress and trade advisory committees. TPA lapsed in July 2007 amidst questions about its use. GAO was asked to review: (1) What FTAs have been pursued under TPA and why? (2) Overall, what is the economic significance of these agreements for the United States? (3) What is the nature of the consultation process for Congress and how well has it worked in practice? (4) What is the nature of the consultation process for trade advisory committees, and how well has it worked in practice? GAO interviewed staff of the Office of the U.S. Trade Representative (USTR), the International Trade Commission (ITC), congressional committees with jurisdiction, trade advisory committees, and others, and reviewed USTR documents.

What GAO Recommends

GAO is making recommendations to USTR and other managing agencies to improve information access and timeliness of congressional consultations, as well as timeliness of rechartering trade advisory committees. GAO also recommends USTR report to Congress on how it meets statutory representation requirements in advisory committee composition. In addition, Congress should consider extending the deadlines for advisory committee and ITC reports by 15 days.

What GAO Found

In the 5-year period that TPA was granted to the President, from 2002-2007, the United States pursued 17 FTAs with 47 countries for a variety of foreign and economic policy reasons. Six FTAs have been approved and are in force, and negotiations for another 4 FTAs have been concluded. The United States has simultaneously pursued comprehensive, high-standard trade agreements on the bilateral and multilateral levels.

Trade with countries for which FTAs were pursued under TPA comprises about 16 percent of U.S. trade and foreign direct investment. Twenty-seven percent of U.S. trade is with countries with FTAs in force prior to TPA (e.g., Canada and Mexico); 56 percent is with countries with which the United States does not have FTAs. The largest U.S. trade partners not pursued under TPA are the European Union, Japan, and China; the rest account for relatively small shares of U.S. trade.

USTR held 1,605 consultations with congressional committee staff from August 2002 through April 2007, but satisfaction with the consultations was mixed. About two-thirds of these meetings were with the House and Senate trade and agriculture committees. Almost all the congressional staff GAO contacted viewed the consultations as providing good information, but slightly more than half said that they did not provide opportunities for real input or influence. These staff often said that they were not given sufficient time to provide meaningful input.

The trade advisory committee chairs GAO contacted said that USTR and managing agencies consulted with their committees fairly regularly, although process issues at times hindered some from functioning effectively. For example, about half said that the 30-day deadline for reporting on the likely impact of FTAs can be difficult to meet, and the ITC had a similar problem. In addition, adherence to statutory representation requirements is not always transparent. Several committees have not been able to meet while their charters were expired, or members had not been reappointed. However, USTR and managing agencies are not required to report to Congress such lapses in a committee's ability to meet.

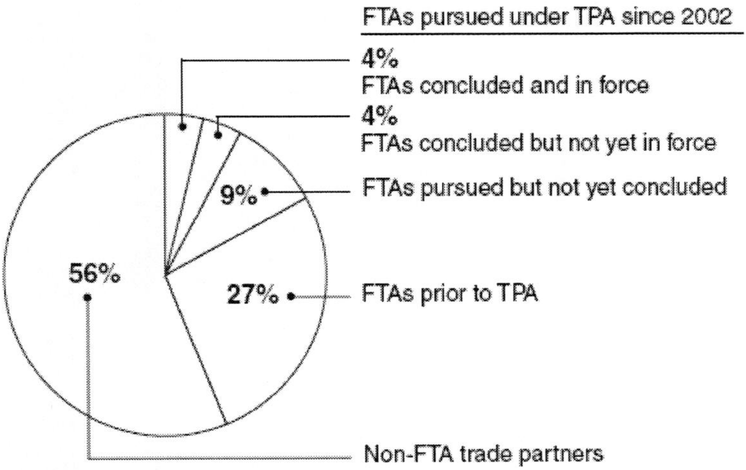

Source: GAO analysis of official U.S. trade statistics from the U.S. Census Bureau.

Figure. Total U.S. Trade by Status of FTA Negotiations under TPA as of 2006.

ABBREVIATIONS

ACTPN	Advisory Committee for Trade Policy and Negotiations
APAC	Agricultural Policy Advisory Committee
ATAC	Agricultural Technical Advisory Committee
CAFTA-DR	Central America – Dominican Republic Free Trade Agreement
COG	Congressional Oversight Group
EU	European Union
FACA	Federal Advisory Committee Act
FTA	Free trade agreement
FTAA	Free Trade Area of the Americas
IGPAC	Intergovernmental Policy Advisory Committee
ITAC	Industry Trade Advisory Committee
ITC	U.S.International Trade Commission
LAC	Labor Advisory Committee
NAFTA	North American Free Trade Agreement
SACU	Southern African Customs Union
TACA	Trade Advisory Committee on Africa
TEPAC	Trade and Environment Policy Advisory Committee
TPA	Trade Promotion Authority
USTR	Office of the U.S. Trade Representative
WTO	World Trade Organization

Chapter 1

INTRODUCTION

Congress granted the President Trade Promotion Authority (TPA) in 2002 through the Trade Act of 2002[1] to negotiate agreements, including free trade agreements (FTA), which aim to reduce trade barriers and expand trade with selected trade partners. The legislation granting TPA stipulated trade negotiating objectives and procedural steps to guide the administration in these negotiations. These include mandatory consultations before, during, and after negotiations with Congress, as well as reports on the likely impact of trade agreements from the formal trade advisory committee system. This congressionally created trade advisory committee system, which includes both policy-level and technical committees, also provides ongoing advice throughout negotiations.

TPA authority lapsed in July 2007, amidst questions about how this authority was used, the economic significance of the FTAs pursued, and the conduct of required consultations before, during, and after negotiations. Yet, the World Trade Organization's (WTO) Doha round of talks aimed at liberalizing trade on a worldwide basis,[2] as well as FTA negotiations with Malaysia, are still ongoing, prompting the President to urge Congress to renew TPA.

To address these issues, we reviewed: (1) What FTAs have been pursued under TPA and why? (2) Overall, what is the economic significance of these agreements to the United States? (3) What is the nature of the consultation process for Congress and how well has it worked in practice? (4) What is the nature of the consultation process for private sector trade advisory committees and other stakeholders, and how well has it worked in practice? As agreed, we will provide a second report in spring 2008 that will provide more information and analysis on the economic and commercial significance of FTAs, as well as a review of progress made by FTA partner countries in strengthening labor and environmental laws and enforcement.

To answer these questions, we reviewed documents and interviewed officials responsible for international trade policy and negotiations at the Office of the U.S. Trade Representative (USTR); the Departments of Agriculture, Commerce, Labor, State, and the Treasury; and the Environmental Protection Agency, as well as officials of the U.S. International Trade Commission (ITC). In addition, to determine what FTAs have been pursued under TPA and why, we reviewed USTR documents and interagency memoranda discussing FTA partner selection and updated our findings from prior GAO work on FTA partner selection.[3] To determine the potential economic and commercial significance of these FTAs, we analyzed official U.S. trade and investment data, as well as studies and analyses from USTR, Commerce, ITC, and trade experts. To determine the nature of the congressional consultation process and how well it has worked in practice, we reviewed consultation provisions from the Trade Act of 1974 up through the Trade Act of 2002,[4] analyzed USTR's congressional consultation logs, and interviewed current and former staff of USTR and the congressional committees that had participated in these consultation meetings. In our congressional interviews, we interviewed House and Senate committees, including majority and minority staffs, of the trade, agriculture, and other committees of jurisdiction. To determine the nature of the consultation process for the trade advisory committees and how well it worked in practice, we reviewed relevant provisions in the Trade Act of 1974,[5] the Federal Advisory Committee Act (FACA),[6] and TPA[7]; analyzed meeting records, charter information, and committee rosters; and interviewed 16 of the relevant 27 trade advisory committee chairs, judgmentally selected from the policy and technical levels of the system, as well as select committee members referred to us by the chairs, and the agency officials responsible for overseeing these committees. We also updated findings from prior GAO work on the trade advisory committees.[8] We conducted our work from January 2007 through August 2007 in accordance with generally accepted government auditing standards. (See appendix I for details about our objectives, scope, and methodology.)

Chapter 2

RESULTS IN BRIEF

In the 5-year period that the President was granted TPA, the United States pursued 17 FTAs with 47 countries for a variety of foreign and economic policy reasons. Since 2002, 6 FTAs have been approved and are in force.[9] Negotiations for another 4 FTAs have been concluded. Strengthening strategic relationships and promoting reform in partner countries are two examples of foreign policy goals that influenced FTA partner selection. Economic policy decision factors included forming regional and subregional trading groups in key regions of the world market and replacing one-way U.S. trade preference programs with two-way reciprocal agreements. In order to further trade liberalization amid lagging WTO talks, the United States simultaneously pursued trade agreements with a number of partners on the bilateral, regional, and global stage as part of a strategy originally referred to as “competitive liberalization” and more recently as “complementary liberalization.” The United States also followed a strategy of pursuing comprehensive and uniformly high standard FTAs, based on TPA negotiating goals, foreign and economic policy considerations, and private sector input. A number of large trading partners such as the European Union (EU), Switzerland, and Japan have not been considered ready to enter into FTA negotiations with the United States because of its requirement that the FTA include agriculture and other sensitive industries or issues, such as services or intellectual property rights. Other partners were not considered ready for FTAs because they were not WTO members or had only recently acceded.

Trade with countries for which FTAs were pursued under TPA comprise about 16 percent of U.S. trade and about 16 percent of U.S. foreign direct investment.[10] Of the 16 percent of trade with partners pursued under TPA, about half is covered by FTAs that are now in force or have been concluded.

These FTAs provide reciprocal access to trade partners' markets and more competitive access for U.S. exporters. Several FTA partners pursued under TPA already had special access to the U.S. market through U.S. trade preference programs, which are unilateral and do not give U.S. exporters preferential duty-free access to foreign beneficiary markets. FTAs address this disparity. Also, while reduction or elimination of trade barriers through FTAs has been estimated to create an overall net economic benefit for the United States and its FTA partners, most economic studies find the gains for the United States of the completed FTAs to be relatively small compared with the overall U.S. economy. Trade with countries not pursued under TPA accounts for about 84 percent of U.S. trade, of which 27 percent is with countries covered by FTAs in force prior to TPA (e.g., Canada and Mexico), and 56 percent is with countries with which the United States does not have FTAs. The largest U.S. trade partners not pursued under TPA are the EU, Japan, and China. Remaining trade partners not pursued under TPA individually account for relatively small shares of U.S. trade.

USTR held extensive consultations with congressional committee staff on FTA negotiations, but satisfaction with those consultations was mixed. USTR held 1,605 consultation meetings with Congress related to FTAs from August 2002 through April 2007. Just over half of these meetings were with the two main trade committees, House Ways and Means and Senate Finance, with another 17 percent with the House and Senate Agriculture Committees, so that about two-thirds of USTR's consultations were with these four committees. Almost all the congressional staff we contacted viewed the consultations as a good conduit for information flow from USTR. However, satisfaction with the quality of the consultations was mixed. While slightly less than half of the staff we interviewed were satisfied with the quality of consultations, slightly more than half believed that the consultations did not provide the opportunity for meaningful input or influence into trade negotiations. A particular concern of many of these staff, especially those not on the trade or agriculture committees, was that the timing of the consultations was often too late to provide meaningful input. Several staff also expressed concern that USTR had not always fully informed them of important changes in the draft text of agreements, which led to controversy in several cases. Various process issues were also raised as concerns to some, including how and to what extent Congress was involved in selection of FTA partners and whether the newly-created Congressional Oversight Group (COG), a bicameral institution involving Members from all committees of jurisdiction, was effective. Congressional staff and former USTR negotiators both agreed on the need to get Congress to focus on trade agreements earlier in the process. USTR officials also said that if more congressional staff working on FTAs under negotiation obtained security clearances, it would greatly facilitate the consultation process.

The private sector advisory committee chairs we contacted said that USTR and the relevant executive branch agencies consulted with the committees on a fairly regular basis, although process issues at times made it difficult for some committees to function effectively. For example, half of the committee chairs we interviewed said that the 30-day deadline for reporting to the President and Congress on the likely impact of final trade agreements[11] can be difficult to meet for several reasons, including sometimes not getting the full text of the agreement from USTR until several days into the 30-day period that officially starts when the President notifies Congress of his or her intent to enter into an FTA.[12] Officials at the ITC reported a similar problem associated with the statutory deadline for its report. In addition, several committee chairs expressed the perception that the composition of their committees was not optimal, either favoring one type of industry or group over another or industry over nonbusiness interests. At the same time, while Congress mandates that the advisory committee system is to involve representative segments of the private sector (e.g., industry, agriculture, and labor and environmental groups), adherence to these statutory requirements[13] is not always transparent. Furthermore, several committees have not been able to meet for periods of time, either because agencies allowed their charters to lapse or had not started the process of soliciting and appointing members soon enough to ensure committees could meet once they were rechartered. The Labor Advisory Committee, for example, did not meet for over 2 years from September 2003 until November 2005 due in part to delays in the member appointment process. USTR and managing agencies, however, are not required to report such lapses in a committee's ability to meet and the reasons behind them.

In this report, we recommend that USTR and other managing agencies improve the timeliness of congressional consultation meetings and the trade advisory committee rechartering and appointment processes. We also recommend that USTR work with Congress to improve access to information prior to consultation meetings. In addition, we recommend USTR report to Congress on any lapses in trade advisory committees' ability to meet, as well as how they meet statutory representation requirements in the composition of the advisory committees. Further, we provide a matter for congressional consideration to extend the deadline of the trade advisory committee and ITC reports by 15 days. We provided a draft of this report to USTR; the Departments of Agriculture, Commerce, Labor, State, and the Treasury; the Environmental Protection Agency; and ITC. The Department of Commerce provided written comments, in which it said that the report was generally an accurate summation of the status and impacts of FTAs and provided a good overview of some of the complexities associated with negotiating an FTA. These comments are reproduced in appendix V. USTR; the Departments of Agriculture, Commerce, and Labor; the Environmental Protection Agency, and ITC provided us with technical comments, which we have incorporated where appropriate. The Departments of State and the Treasury had no comments. USTR staff also commented to GAO on the proposed recommendations regarding statutory representation requirements in advisory committee composition and consultation with Congress. GAO incorporated these comments as appropriate in the final report. USTR indicated that it would report on the actions taken in response to the recommendations in a letter as required under U.S. law.

Chapter 3

BACKGROUND

In 2002, Congress passed legislation renewing the President's ability to enter into certain trade agreements and submit implementing bills[14] on an expedited legislative track without possibility of amendment. The bill granting this "fast track" authority, renamed TPA, passed the House by one vote amid contentious debate, with a noticeable split along party lines. Although delegation of the constitutional authority to "regulate commerce with foreign nations" dates back to 1934[15] and some form of fast track authority was granted by Congress to every president since 1974,[16] the Bipartisan Trade Promotion Authority Act of 2002 restored this authority after an 8-year hiatus.

Congress accompanied this grant with statutorily defined objectives for the trade negotiations and requirements that the administration consult with Congress and other stakeholders before, during, and after the negotiations.[17] If Congress decided that the President hadn't satisfied his or her obligations to consult under TPA, the implementing legislation could be treated like any other bill. Congress has applied TPA procedures to every implementing bill submitted under the Trade Act, according to USTR. Additional information about the history of the consultation requirements can be found in appendix II.

TPA also requires the administration to consult with private sector advisory committees.[18] It continues the advisory committee system established under the Trade Act of 1974, which was intended to ensure that representatives from private business and other groups with a stake in trade policy could provide input before, during, and after negotiations. The system has a three-tier structure of committees to advise the President on (1) overall trade policy, (2) general policy areas, and (3) technical aspects of trade agreements. The law requires the President to consult with these committees on a continuing and timely basis.[19] Each advisory committee must submit a report to Congress and the President on each trade agreement negotiated under TPA no later than 30 days after the President notifies Congress of his or her intent to enter into the agreement.[20] The system comprises about 700 advisors across 28 committees broadly representative of the U.S. economy and various trade policy interests.

The Trade Act of 1974 also requires USTR to provide an opportunity to private organizations or groups outside the advisory committee system to present their views on trade issues.[21] To comply with this requirement, USTR publishes a *Federal Register* notice and the Trade Policy Staff Committee[22] conducts a hearing. The public can comment on any matter relevant to the proposed agreement in response to the *Federal Register* notice, either in writing or at the public hearing. USTR also consults with groups outside of these mechanisms; sometimes USTR is contacted, and sometimes USTR seeks out comments.

We reported on the trade advisory committee system in 2002 and found that it has made valuable contributions to U.S. trade policy and agreements.[23] We also found, however, that consultations were not always timely or useful and that the process needed greater accountability. Furthermore, we found that committee structure and composition had not been updated to reflect changes in the U.S. economy and trade policy. In response to these findings, USTR and the other managing agencies have taken several actions, including the installation of a secure Web site for viewing draft agreement text; reconfiguration of the committee system; introduction of a monthly teleconference of chairs; and introduction of periodic plenary sessions for the third tier technical committees.

TPA was actively used by the President. In addition to pursuing numerous FTAs, a global round of trade liberalization talks at the WTO launched in November 2001 was subsequently notified under TPA. WTO talks made some progress, but they were not concluded by the July 1, 2007, deadline TPA set for an agreement to qualify. The President has called on Congress to renew TPA, in part to continue pursuit of WTO talks in hopes of achieving fundamental global agriculture reform and meaningful reduction in trade barriers to goods and services worldwide. Some in Congress are supportive, but others are skeptical, making an examination of recent experience under TPA timely. Meanwhile, FTA negotiations with Malaysia have continued despite the lapse in TPA. Congress must also decide whether to approve the last four FTAs concluded under TPA—with Peru, Colombia, Panama, and South Korea.

Chapter 4

Since Passage of TPA, the United States Has Pursued Negotiations of 17 Comprehensive FTAs for Foreign and Economic Policy Reasons

Since the passage of TPA in 2002, the United States has pursued negotiations towards 17 comprehensive FTAs covering 47 countries. FTA partner countries were selected for a variety of foreign and economic policy reasons. The United States followed a strategy of competitive liberalization, which entails simultaneously pursuing bilateral, multilateral, and global trade agreements. Furthermore, the United States only pursued comprehensive FTAs, but a number of large trading partners were unwilling to negotiate on sensitive topics such as agriculture in FTAs.

Since 2002, the United States Has Pursued Negotiations of 17 FTAs with 47 Countries

In the 5-year period that TPA was granted to the President, from 2002-2007, the administration pursued negotiations toward 17 FTAs with 47 countries.[24] These 47 countries extend from North America to South America to the Pacific Rim to the Middle East. (See table 1.) Six FTAs have been approved and are in force. An additional 4 FTAs with 4 countries have been signed but not yet approved, and FTAs with Costa Rica[25] and Oman have been signed and approved by the U.S. Congress but are not yet in force.[26] Furthermore, an FTA with Malaysia is currently under negotiation, and negotiations for the remaining 5 FTAs are not yet concluded.[27]

Table 1. Free Trade Agreements Negotiated under Trade Promotion Authority

Agreements concluded and in force			
Agreement country	Entry into force		
Singapore	January 1, 2004		
Chile	January 1, 2004		
Australia	January 1, 2005		
Morocco	January 1, 2006		
Central America–Dominican Republic FTA (CAFTA-DR)[a]			
El Salvador	March 1, 2006		
Honduras	April 1, 2006		
Nicaragua	April 1, 2006		
Guatemala	July 1, 2006		
Dominican Republic	March 1, 2007		
Bahrain	August 1, 2006		
Agreements concluded but not yet in force			
Agreement country	Negotiations concluded	Agreement signed	U.S. implementing legislation signed
CAFTA-DR Costa Rica	January 25, 2004	May 28, 2004	August 2, 2005 (Costa Rica government approved, but not yet implemented)
Oman	October 3, 2005	January 19, 2006	September 26, 2006 (Oman government approved, but not yet implemented)
Peru[b]	December 7, 2005	April 12, 2006	Not yet signed
Colombia[b]	February 27, 2006	November 22, 2006	Not yet signed
Panama	December 19, 2006	June 28, 2007	Not yet signed
South Korea	April 1, 2007	June 30, 2007	Not yet signed
Current negotiations			
Negotiation country	**Negotiations began**		
Malaysia	March 8, 2006		

Table 1. (Continued).

Negotiations not yet concluded			
Negotiation country	**Negotiations began**		
Free Trade Area of the Americas (FTAA)[e]	April 19, 1998[c]		
Southern African Customs Union (SACU)[f]	June 2, 2003		
Agreements concluded and in force			
Ecuador[b]	May 18, 2004		
Thailand	June 28, 2004		
United Arab Emirates[d]	March 12, 2005		
Agreements concluded and in force prior to TPA			
Agreement country	**Entry into effect**		
Israel	September 1, 1985		
Canada	January 1, 1989		
North American FTA (NAFTA)			
Canada	January 1, 1994		
Mexico	January 1, 1994		
Jordan	December 17, 2001		

Source: GAO analysis of USTR data.

[a] The Dominican Republic was integrated into CAFTA after CAFTA negotiations had been concluded.

[b] Negotiations with Peru, Colombia, and Ecuador began together on May 18, 2004. Eventually, the Untied States concluded separate bilateral agreements with Peru and Colombia, but not with Ecuador. While Bolivia was an observer at the initial talks, negotiations with Bolivia never got under way.

[c] Negotiations for the FTAA began before TPA was granted, but the United States continued to negotiate it under TPA. At present, however, negotiations for the FTAA are at an impasse.

[d] The United States and the United Arab Emirates have, for the short term, switched their efforts from negotiating an FTA to deepening their economic relationship through their 2004 Trade and Investment Framework Agreement. The long-term objective of both sides, however, remains a comprehensive FTA.

[e] The countries included in the FTAA are: Antigua and Barbuda, Argentina, Bahamas, Barbados, Belize, Bolivia, Brazil, Canada, Chile, Colombia, Costa Rica, Dominica, Dominican Republic, Ecuador, El Salvador, Grenada, Guatemala, Guyana, Haiti, Honduras, Jamaica, Mexico, Nicaragua, Panama, Paraguay, Peru, Saint Kitts and Nevis, Saint Lucia, Saint Vincent and the Grenadines, Suriname, Trinidad and Tobago, Uruguay, and Venezuela.

[f] The countries included in SACU are: Botswana, Lesotho, Namibia, South Africa, and Swaziland.

FTA Partners Were Selected for a Variety of Foreign and Economic Policy Reasons

The United States has negotiated comprehensive FTAs for a variety of foreign and economic policy reasons. Agency officials confirmed that since mid-2004, FTA partners have been judged on six criteria outlined by the National Security Council, as GAO reported in 2004.[28] These criteria are as follows:

- country readiness,
- economic/commercial benefit,
- benefits to the broader trade liberalization strategy,
- compatibility with U.S. interests,
- congressional/private sector support, and
- U.S. government resource constraints.

According to officials we interviewed, these criteria are broad and, as a result, the administration has considerable discretion in choosing potential FTA partners. Among the foreign policy considerations for selecting FTA partners are the strengthening of strategic relationships and the promotion of reform in partner countries. In addition to the first two criteria mentioned above of assessing country readiness as well as the economic/commercial benefit, forming regional trading blocks and replacing trade preference programs were among the economic policy factors.

Strengthening Strategic Relationships

Agency officials told us that establishing trading relationships with strategic friends and allies was a key factor in deciding with whom to enter into FTA negotiations. Particularly following the September 11 terrorist attacks and the onset of the Iraq war, pursuing FTAs with moderate Muslim countries became a significant policy goal. In May 2003, the President announced a Middle East Free Trade Initiative, which lays out a plan of graduated steps for Middle Eastern nations to increase trade and investment with the United States. Under this initiative, the United States has entered into FTAs with Morocco and Bahrain and has approved an FTA with Oman. This is in addition to the FTAs the United States already had with Israel and Jordan. USTR indicated in its November 2004 letter of intent to enter into an FTA with Oman, for example, that Oman, as a member of the Gulf Cooperation Council, will "continue to be an important strategic colleague on a broad array of foreign and national security issues." The United States has sought to strengthen strategic relationships through FTAs in other regions as well. For example, the November 2003 letter of intent to enter into an FTA with Panama indicated that "an FTA will serve to strengthen not only economic ties but also political and security ones."

Promoting Reform in Partner Countries

Another foreign policy goal in selecting FTA partners was promoting economic and political reform in partner countries. Public statements regarding the FTA with Morocco, for example, suggest that it would add momentum to political reform already under way there. USTR also stated that the Central America—Dominican Republic Free Trade Agreement (CAFTA-DR) will strengthen "free-market reforms" in Central America, adding that "the growth stimulated by trade and the openness of an agreement will help deepen democracy, the rule of law, and sustainable development." Public documents related to the Andean FTA initiative state that an Andean FTA would "enhance our efforts to strengthen democracy and support for fundamental values in the region" such as rule of law, sustainable development, transparency, anti-corruption, and good governance. USTR also indicated that an FTA with South Korea would promote enhanced regulatory transparency in a top U.S. trade partner.

Enhancing Regional Economic Initiatives

Beyond assessing a country's readiness and potential economic/commercial benefits, USTR publications and interviews with senior agency officials suggest that sequencing from previous FTAs and building toward larger regional initiatives were considerations for entering into negotiations with a number of countries. For example, as the U.S.-Chile FTA negotiations were drawing to a close, the United States announced its intent to enter into FTA negotiations with the Central American countries of Costa Rica, El Salvador, Guatemala, Honduras, and Nicaragua under CAFTA and later announced its intent to include the Dominican Republic in those negotiations. USTR also submitted a letter of intent to enter into FTA negotiations with the Andean countries of Colombia, Peru, Ecuador, and Bolivia under the Andean FTA. The individual letters of intent to enter in FTA negotiations with these ten countries cited the complementary nature of these negotiations, which would lend momentum to concluding the Free Trade Area of the Americas (FTAA). Agency officials explained that when the United States pursues individual bilateral FTAs, one goal is to enable them to be woven into regional agreements under the mantle of broader integration. The individual letters of intent to enter into FTA negotiations with Thailand and Malaysia also cited the Enterprise for ASEAN Initiative as a factor in the selection process, building upon the U.S.-Singapore FTA. The administration envisioned similar regional or subregional trading groups for the Middle East (the Middle East Free Trade Area) and South Africa (SACU, Southern African Customs Union). (See figure 1.)

Transitioning from Trade Preference Programs

For certain developing country FTA partners, one motivation in U.S. selection was converting one-way U.S. trade preference programs into two-way reciprocal agreements. Agency officials explained that under preference programs such as the Generalized System of Preferences[29] and the Caribbean Basin Initiative,[30] developing countries have preferential duty-free access to the American market without having to reciprocate; by entering into FTAs with them, the United States "levels the playing field" by gaining market access in these countries. Public documents related to the SACU trade negotiations, for example, noted an opportunity to replace the African Growth and Opportunity Act[31] trade preference program with an FTA for several of the partner countries. The Andean FTA was motivated in part by a desire to replace the Andean Trade Preference Agreement,[32] while the CAFTA-DR[33] was motivated in part by a desire to replace a major portion of the Caribbean Basin Initiative. Furthermore, USTR officials noted that transitioning from unilateral trade preferences to reciprocal trade agreements would deepen existing regional integration. USTR identified section 202(b) of the United States-Caribbean Basin Trade Partnership Act[34] as an example of how this evolution was also a goal that Congress shared.

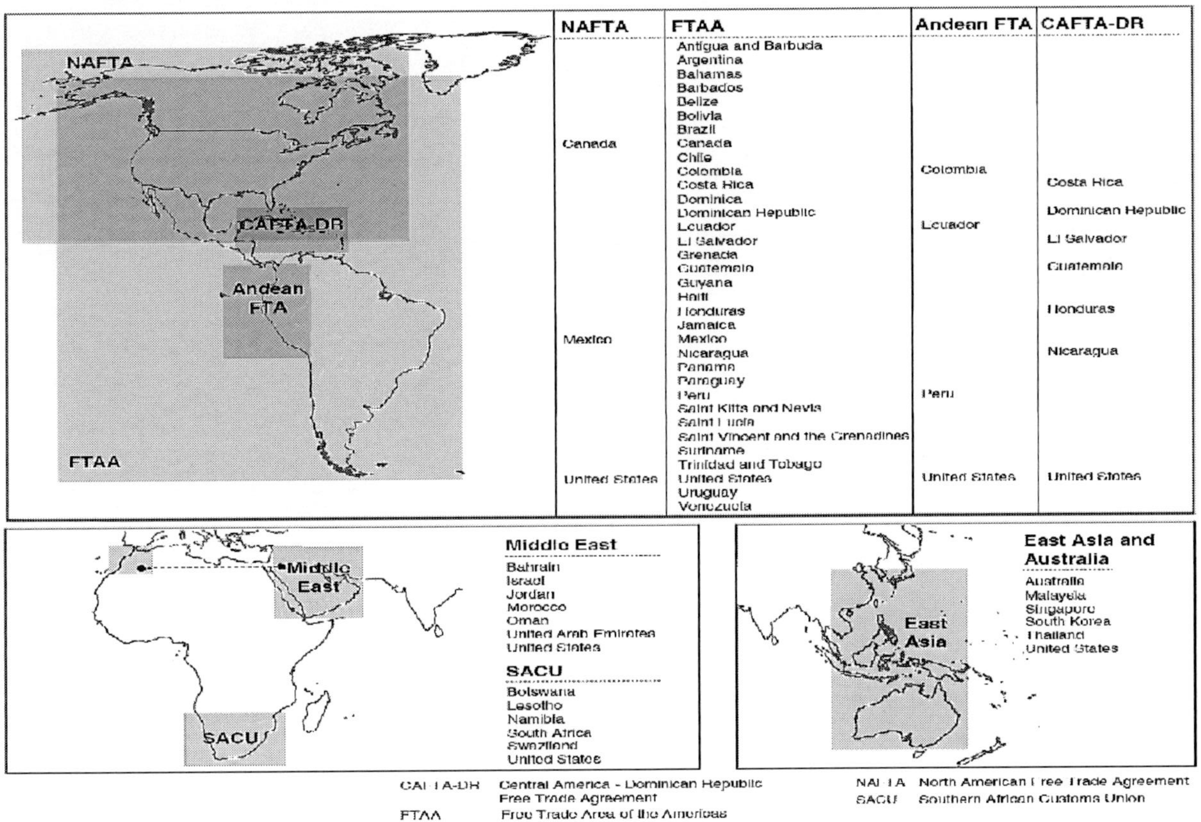

Sources: GAO (data); Map Resources (maps).

Figure 1. Pursuit of a Regional Focus for FTAs.

Under TPA, the Administration Pursued Strategies of Competitive Liberalization and Comprehensive FTAs

As WTO negotiations have repeatedly stalled in the face of wide substantive differences, particularly over agriculture,[35] the United States has sought to continue to be active in pursuing trade agreements at other levels, even prior to TPA. As part of its mission to play the leading role in developing and coordinating U.S. trade policy, USTR pursued trade agreements throughout the 1990s not only at the global level through the WTO, but also at the bilateral and multilateral levels, such as through the U.S.-Jordan FTA and the North American Free Trade Agreement (NAFTA).

Since TPA passage, USTR officials stressed that they would simultaneously pursue bilateral, multilateral, and global trade agreements under a strategy referred to as "competitive liberalization," or more recently as "complementary liberalization." This competitive liberalization strategy linked trade policy to foreign policy, security policy, and commercial policy goals. Although still committed to liberalization on a global front, working in parallel with the WTO framework offered an opportunity to keep the concept of achieving liberalization moving forward despite setbacks at the global level.

Competitive liberalization had the dual goal of providing momentum for global trade liberalization and providing an alternative if global trade talks failed to progress. As former U.S. Trade Representative Robert Zoellick explained in 2002, "we will not passively accept a veto over America's drive to open markets. We want to encourage reformers who favor free trade. If others do not want to move forward, the United States will move ahead with those who do." Agency officials say that, due to its importance to the global trading system and the potential of more significant and broad-based economic gains, the successful completion of global trade agreements such as the WTO Doha Round is the administration's ultimate goal and that FTAs were intended to serve as a stepping stone to that goal since they can provide a substantial demonstration effect. U.S. Trade Representative Susan Schwab said in her May 2006 Senate confirmation hearing that pursuing FTAs helps "to establish the breadth and scope of potential multilateral agreements in years to come by setting precedents and by demonstrating the real benefits of free and fair trade." For example, according to administration officials, signing NAFTA contributed to moving the last (Uruguay) round of global trade talks creating the WTO to conclusion. Additionally, FTAs were seen as a tool to strengthen relationships with trading partners similarly seeking progress in global liberalization. In the letter announcing its intent to negotiate an FTA with Australia, for example, the USTR stated "we believe that an FTA would further unite and strengthen the alliance of countries leading the effort toward global trade liberalization." The second goal of competitive liberalization was to provide an alternative venue for pursuing trade liberalization as WTO talks lagged. However, whereas competitive liberalization sought to pressure other countries to agree to tariff and subsidy cuts in the WTO, complementary liberalization sees the simultaneous pursuit of FTAs and WTO negotiations as a mutually reinforcing effort. Former U.S. Trade Representative Robert Portman explained in 2006 that, "where we have a free trade agreement, we find we have...the ability to have a better relationship on the multilateral issues [and] it's relatively easy on the global stage...to find some solutions."

Closely tied to the strategy of competitive/complementary liberalization is the strategy of pursuing only highly comprehensive "gold standard" bilateral and regional FTAs. Such agreements have a number of absolute requirements, based on the model USTR seeks to use. NAFTA was the original "model," although requirements have evolved with time and with different regions. USTR insists, for example, that partners accept the inclusion of agriculture, as well as a "negative list" approach to services,[36] because they believe this will provide greater liberalization and lessen impediments to securing market access. Agency officials did say there is some room to change specific language depending on a country's individual needs, such as changing what level of market access would be proposed, and the timetable for phasing down barriers. However, officials also noted that taking products, sectors, or issues off the table, particularly ones such as intellectual property rights that are considered to provide a U.S. competitive advantage, generally precludes or creates an impasse in negotiations. Other countries that negotiate FTAs frequently exclude sensitive industries or issues. Some trade experts argued that USTR's pursuit of comprehensive agreements limits potential FTA partners since a number of larger economies are unwilling to enter into such comprehensive negotiations. Administration officials recognized this and cited the EU, Switzerland, and Japan as examples of major trading partners with which an FTA with the United States could have significant commercial value but where the trading partner appears unwilling to assume obligations consistent with the objectives set out in TPA. USTR reports that it paused negotiations pursued under TPA with other large countries or subregions, such as the FTAA and SACU, in part for similar reasons. At the same time, some partners were not considered ready for FTAs because they either were not WTO members or had only recently acceded.

Agency officials told us that a number of interrelated factors influenced their decision to pursue exclusively comprehensive trade agreements:

- *Legislative requirements*–Agency officials told us that TPA legislation played a large role in the decision to pursue only comprehensive FTAs. Since, under TPA, each agreement must make progress in meeting the applicable negotiating objectives prescribed by Congress,[37] USTR only pursues FTAs in which the negotiating objectives are translated into 16 standard chapter headings, and the provisions require partner countries to pursue a number of nontariff based reforms. These include transparency in government procurement, protection from discrimination for investors, and liberalization of financial and other services. Agency officials told us that USTR has some discretion in how to pursue these objectives, but since the objectives are statutorily mandated, their discretion starts at a fairly high bar.
- *Foreign and economic policy goals*–The administration has said that pursuing comprehensive FTAs links trade policy to foreign policy and security policy goals. According to USTR, comprehensive FTAs include a number of provisions linking the trade agreement to other goals such as encouraging reform and openness, strengthening partners' regulatory environments, and establishing the framework for promoting democracy. Furthermore, agency officials and trade experts stressed that if the United States pursued FTAs with "sweetheart exemptions" it would actually be undermining the international trading system in violation of WTO rules and regulations. Furthermore, agency officials questioned whether pursuing noncomprehensive FTAs would lead to noticeable commercial gains since trade barriers with large trading partners usually only remain in sensitive industries.
- *Private sector input*–Since all trade agreements must be approved by Congress, USTR officials told us they only negotiate agreements that they think will receive broad domestic support. As private sector representatives have identified certain "deal breakers," which must be included in order to gain their support, USTR officials always include these topics in the FTAs they negotiate. These topics include a negative lists approach to services and inclusion of intellectual property protection provisions.
- *Negotiating strategy*–Agency officials and congressional staff involved in trade issues also told us that since the precedent that the United States only engages in comprehensive FTAs has been set, they have reinforced their credibility in insisting on future comprehensive FTAs. Partner countries also have a better sense of what the United States expects. A trade expert we spoke with added that due to the asymmetric bargaining

> strength of the United States compared with most of its negotiating partners given the relative sizes of their economies, USTR likely has more leverage in proposing the baseline agreement for the negotiation. On the other hand, the United States has had less success in insisting on such requirements with some large prospective partners, such as Brazil, Switzerland, and Japan.

Not everyone involved in trade negotiations, however, believes that exclusively pursuing comprehensive FTAs is in the best interest of the United States. We heard from both the private sector and former congressional staff that strict insistence on comprehensive FTAs may disadvantage the United States compared with other countries that engage in FTAs more liberally. In addition, they told us that "one size does not fit all" and developing countries need help to develop before they trade with the United States. Agency officials told us, however, that due to the factors listed above, they remain convinced that pursuing comprehensive FTAs is the best policy for the United States. Furthermore, they pointed out that a prospective FTA partner's readiness to undertake obligations which would meet TPA objectives and U.S. interests is evaluated in the selection choice. If a country or group of countries is not ready, the United States uses other mechanisms such as Trade and Investment Framework Agreements as building blocks, including capacity building.

Chapter 5

FTAs Pursued Account for Limited Share of U.S. Trade and Investment but Include Diverse Markets for U.S. Exports

Trade with countries for which FTAs were pursued under TPA accounted for about 16 percent of U.S. trade in 2006 and about 16 percent of U.S. foreign direct investment in 2005. FTAs seek to expand opportunities for U.S. exporters in foreign markets, while solidifying the trade and investment relationship with these trade partners. Of the remaining 84 percent of U.S. trade, 27 percent was with countries for which the U.S. had an FTA prior to TPA (e.g., Canada and Mexico) and 56 percent was with countries not pursued under TPA, including the EU, Japan, and China.

FTAs Pursued Account for about 16 Percent of U.S. Trade

Of the approximately $3.4 trillion in U.S. trade in 2006, FTAs pursued under TPA accounted for about $558 billion, or 16 percent of the total. This includes exports and imports and both goods and services. About half of this trade (8 percent) was accounted for by agreements in force or concluded; the remainder was with partners with whom the United States has not yet concluded an agreement. Figure 2 shows the breakdown of total U.S. trade (exports plus imports of goods and services) across groups of trade partners.

Table 2. U.S. Trade (Goods and Services) with All U.S. Trade Partners

U.S. dollars in millions				
Partners	**Total trade**	**Share of total**	**Share of exports**	**Share of imports**
FTAs pursued under TPA	558,276	16%	19%	15%
FTAs concluded and in force	136,082	4	6	3
FTAs concluded but not yet in force	128,304	4	4	3
FTAs pursued but not yet concluded	293,890	9	9	8
FTAs prior to TPA	937,092	27	29	26
Non-FTA trade partners	1,920,223	56	52	59
Total	3,415,591	100%	100%	100%

Sources: GAO analysis of official U.S. trade statistics from the U.S. Census Bureau and the Bureau of Economic Analysis.

Notes: U.S. trade in goods statistics from 2006; U.S. trade in services statistics from 2005 (most recent year available). Percentages do not always total 100 percent due to rounding.

Services trade data was not available individually for some countries if they were not large suppliers or purchasers of services products. See appendix III, table 6, for services trade by country, which indicates whether trade data was available.

Goods trade statistics are imports for consumption (customs value) and domestic exports (free alongside ship (FAS) value).

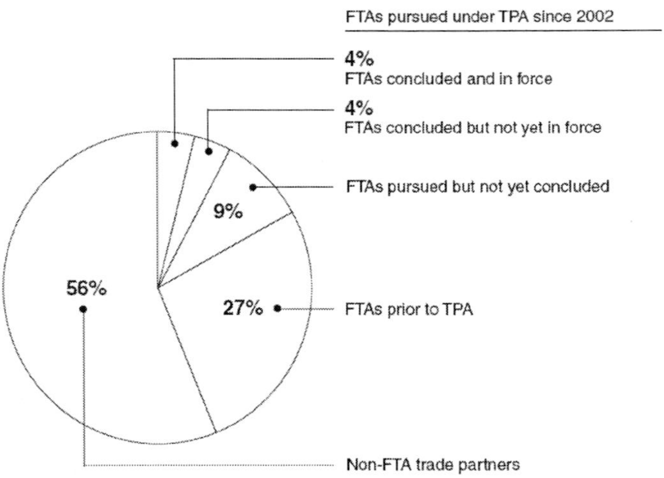

Source: GAO analysis of official U.S. trade statistics from the U.S. Census Bureau.

Notes: Percentages for FTAs pursued under TPA actually add to 16 percent but do not total due to rounding.

See table 2 for data and analysis used.

Figure 2. Total U.S. Trade by Status of FTA Negotiations under TPA.

FTAs pursued under TPA accounted for a somewhat larger share of total U.S. exports (19 percent) than U.S. imports (15 percent). This pattern is reversed with non-FTA countries, which accounted for 52 percent of U.S. exports, but 59 percent of U.S. imports. Table 2 shows the share of overall U.S. trade, exports, and imports by status of FTA negotiations under TPA. In addition, countries with which the United States pursued FTAs accounted for about 16 percent of U.S. foreign direct investment in 2005 (see app. III for more information on U.S. foreign direct investment).

Countries with which the United States has pursued FTAs under TPA are a diverse group. Table 3 shows the countries pursued by the status of the FTA negotiations. Concluded agreements already in force include countries in Asia (Australia and Singapore), the Middle East and North Africa (Bahrain and Morocco), and Latin America (Chile and CAFTA-DR[38]). The concluded agreement with South Korea, for which implementing legislation has not yet been submitted to Congress, would account for the single largest individual trade partner of those pursued under TPA (about 3 percent of total U.S. trade). However, the FTAA, for which negotiations are at an impasse, would have encompassed the largest economic area since it includes Brazil and Argentina, as well as existing FTA partners in NAFTA (Canada and Mexico), CAFTA-DR, Chile, and others in the Western Hemisphere.

Table 3. U.S. Trade (Goods and Services) for FTAs Pursued under TPA

U.S. dollars in millions				
Partners	**Total trade**	**Share of total**	**Share of exports**	**Share of imports**
All countries	3,415,591	100.0%	100.0%	100.0%
All FTAs under TPA	558,276	16.3	19.2	14.6
FTAs concluded and in force	136,082	4.0	5.9	2.8
Australia	37,149	1.1	1.9	0.6
Bahrain	1,103	0.0	0.0	0.0
Singapore	49,141	1.4	2.1	1.0
Chile	17,837	0.5	0.6	0.5
Morocco	1,416	0.0	0.1	0.0
CAFTA-DR	29,437	0.9	1.1	0.7
Dominican Republic	9,573	0.3	0.4	0.2
El Salvador	3,926	0.1	0.2	0.1
Guatemala	6,401	0.2	0.3	0.1
Honduras	7,306	0.2	0.3	0.2
Nicaragua	2,231	0.1	0.1	0.1
FTAs concluded but not yet in force	128,304	3.8	4.4	3.3
Colombia	15,475	0.5	0.5	0.4

Table 3. Continued.

U.S. dollars in millions				
Partners	**Total trade**	**Share of total**	**Share of exports**	**Share of imports**
Costa Rica	7,691	0.2	0.3	0.2
Oman	1,614	0.0	0.1	0.0
Panama	2,861	0.1	0.2	0.0
Peru	8,552	0.3	0.2	0.3
South Korea	92,111	2.7	3.2	2.4
FTAs pursued but not yet concluded	293,890	8.6	8.9	8.4
FTAA	184,068	5.4	5.9	5.1
Brazil	51,074	1.5	1.8	1.3
Argentina	10,800	0.3	0.5	0.2
Venezuela	47,977	1.4	0.9	1.7
Ecuador	9,560	0.3	0.2	0.3
Other	64,657	1.9	2.6	1.5
Thailand	32,469	1.0	0.7	1.1
Malaysia	49,685	1.5	1.0	1.7
United Arab Emirates	12,511	0.4	0.9	0.1
SACU	15,156	0.4	0.5	0.4
Botswana	279	0.0	0.0	0.0
Lesotho	412	0.0	0.0	0.0
Namibia	229	0.0	0.0	0.0
South Africa	14,069	0.4	0.4	0.4
Swaziland	167	0.0	0.0	0.0
FTAs prior to TPA	**937,092**	**27.4**	**29.3**	**26.3**
Israel	32,363	0.9	0.8	1.0
Jordan	2,045	0.1	0.0	0.1
NAFTA	902,684	26.4	28.4	25.3
Canada	555,789	16.3	17.9	15.3
Mexico	346,896	10.2	10.5	10.0
Non-FTA countries	**1,920,223**	**56.2**	**51.6**	**59.0**
EU	761,921	22.3	25.2	20.5
Japan	267,768	7.8	7.6	8.0
China	354,260	10.4	4.7	13.8
India	40,910	1.2	1.1	1.3
All others	495,365	14.5%	13.0%	15.4%

Legend: CAFTA-DR = Central America-Dominican Republic Free Trade Agreement FTAA = Free Trade Area of the Americas NAFTA = North American Free Trade Agreement SACU = Southern African Customs Union

Sources: GAO analysis of official U.S. trade statistics from the U.S. Census Bureau and the Bureau of Economic Analysis.

Notes: U.S. trade in goods statistics are for 2006; U.S. trade in services statistics are for 2005, which is the most recent year available. "0.0%" are values less than 0.05 percent which round to zero. Percentages do not always total 100 percent due to rounding.

Services trade data was not available individually for some countries if they were not large suppliers or purchasers of services products. See appendix III, table 6, for services trade by country, which indicates whether trade data was available.

FTAs Provide Permanent, Reciprocal Access for U.S. Trade and Competitive Playing Field for U.S. Exports

The FTAs pursued under TPA seek a high level of liberalization. As noted previously, the United States has sought elimination of substantially all trade barriers under its FTAs in order to maximize the overall economic benefits of the agreements. While reduction or elimination of trade barriers through FTAs has been estimated to create an overall net economic benefit for the United States and its FTA partners, most economic studies find the gains for the United States of the FTAs to be relatively small compared with the overall U.S. economy.[39] Assessments by ITC of economy-wide and sectoral effects of actual, completed FTAs also indicate positive but generally small effects on the U.S. economy and trade overall. (The U.S. FTA with South Korea is predicted to have modest effects.) However, with the exception of Singapore, given the FTA partners' generally higher trade barriers, U.S. export gains are predicted to be larger than import increases for each FTA the ITC has assessed. For South Korea, U.S. exports are predicted to rise by $9.7 to 10.9 billion, while U.S. imports from South Korea rise by $6.4 to $6.9 billion.[40]

While FTAs require the United States to lower its trade barriers, several FTA partners pursued under TPA already had special access to the U.S. market through U.S. trade preference programs. For example, CAFTA-DR economies had preferential access to the U.S. market through the Generalized System of Preferences and the Caribbean Basin Initiative (including the Caribbean Basin Trade Promotion Act, which provided additional access). However, FTAs provide superior market access for several reasons. First, product coverage under FTAs is more complete. About 91 percent of products in the U.S. tariff schedule (for goods) are either eligible for preferential access (54 percent) or are already duty-free for most countries (37 percent). The remaining 9 percent of products are still dutiable even for countries eligible for preference programs. FTAs eliminate nearly all U.S. duties on these remaining products. Second, FTAs are bilateral agreements that provide trade partners with permanent access to the U.S. market. Preference programs are unilateral programs that need reauthorization.[41] Lapses in authorization have created uncertainty in the past for both foreign exporters and investors. Finally, since preference programs are unilateral, U.S. exporters do not receive preferential duty-free access to foreign beneficiary markets. FTAs address this disparity.

FTAs also help U.S. exports maintain a competitive advantage or counteract the advantages of third-country competitors that may already have better access to foreign markets through their own FTAs. In cases in which competitors do not have an FTA with U.S. FTA partners, U.S. exports gain an advantage over exports from competitors. The edge varies by country and product and depends on the restrictiveness of the tariff and nontariff barriers in our FTA partners' economies. For example, in CAFTA-DR countries, the simple average tariff rate across all products ranged from 5.6 to 8.5 percent in 2006, with tariffs on agricultural products ranging from 9.7 to 13.1 percent.[42] Non-FTA countries must still pay these rates on their exports. U.S. "most favored nation" tariff rates,[43] which apply to all but two U.S. partners (North Korea and Cuba) that do not otherwise qualify for special, lower, rates, by comparison, were 3.5 percent overall and 5.3 percent for agricultural products. In some countries, average most favored nation tariff rates are even higher on agricultural products relative to those on nonagricultural products. For example, according to the WTO,[44] the overall average tariff rate for South Korea on all products was 12.1 percent, but 47.8 percent for agricultural products. Table 8 in appendix III shows the simple average tariff rates (non-FTA rates) across U.S. FTA partners to provide an indication of the tariff benefits provided by FTAs. For countries that have FTAs with trade partners besides the United States, FTAs help restore the competitiveness of U.S. exports by providing comparable access. For example, Chile also has FTAs with Canada, Mexico, and the EU, as well as the United States. If the United States did not have an FTA with Chile, then U.S. exporters would be at a disadvantage relative to exporters from Canada, Mexico, and the EU. On the other hand, since FTA partners are free to enter into additional agreement with other countries, any advantage gained for U.S. exporters may be temporary.

MAJORITY OF TRADE ALREADY COVERED BY FTAS PRIOR TO TPA OR NOT PURSUED UNDER TPA

Non-FTA trade partners accounted for over half (56 percent) of U.S. trade in 2006. The remaining share of U.S. trade was accounted for by countries pursued under TPA (16 percent) and countries with which the United States already had an existing FTA (27 percent). Of the non-FTA trade partners, some of them comprised relatively large shares of U.S. trade. Table 4 shows the top 20 markets for U.S. exports and top 20 suppliers of U.S. imports among non-FTA trade partners. The largest market and supplier—the EU with its current 27 member countries—accounted for approximately 21 percent of U.S. exports and nearly 18 percent of U.S. imports. Japan, China, and Taiwan were the next 3 largest markets and suppliers for the United States, although China is the second largest non-FTA supplier after the EU.

Table 4. Top 20 Non-FTA Trade Partners, Goods Exports and Imports, 2006

U.S. dollars in millions							
Rank	Trade partner	Exports 2006	Share of exports 2006	Rank	Trade partner	Imports 2006	Share of imports 2006
1.	EU-27	197,281	21.2%	1.	EU-27	330,898	17.9%
2.	Japan	55,596	6.0	2.	China	287,052	15.6
3.	China	51,624	5.6	3.	Japan	148,071	8.0
4.	Taiwan	21,376	2.3	4.	Taiwan	38,086	2.1
5.	Hong Kong	13,395	1.4	5.	Saudi Arabia	31,142	1.7
6.	Switzerland	11,597	1.2	6.	Nigeria	27,863	1.5
7.	India	9,025	1.0	7.	India	21,674	1.2
8.	Philippines	7,304	0.8	8.	Russia	19,642	1.1
9.	Saudi Arabia	7,262	0.8	9.	Algeria	14,753	0.8
10.	Turkey	5,524	0.6	10.	Switzerland	14,174	0.8
11.	Russia	4,215	0.5	11.	Indonesia	13,268	0.7
12.	Egypt	4,061	0.4	12.	Angola	11,514	0.6
13.	Indonesia	3,015	0.3	13.	Iraq	11,326	0.6
14.	New Zealand	2,802	0.3	14.	Philippines	9,697	0.5
15.	Norway	2,259	0.2	15.	Vietnam	8,463	0.5
16.	Nigeria	2,146	0.2	16.	Hong Kong	7,921	0.4
17.	Pakistan	1,962	0.2	17.	Norway	6,852	0.4
18.	Kuwait	1,948	0.2	18.	Turkey	5,387	0.3
19.	Angola	1,543	0.2	19.	Kuwait	3,903	0.2
20.	Iraq	1,456	0.2%	20.	Pakistan	3,667	0.2%

Source: GAO analysis of official U.S. statistics from the U.S. Census Bureau.

There are several reasons why the United States has chosen not to pursue some of the largest trade partners for FTA negotiations. As discussed previously, the United States seeks to include agricultural liberalization in its FTA agreements. This is a sensitive issue with the EU that is also being dealt with at the WTO and has made prospects for a U.S.-EU FTA less likely. Since trade barriers on nonagricultural products between the U.S. and EU are already very low, an FTA that did not include agriculture would have less impact. Similarly, agriculture issues are sensitive with Japan and Switzerland. However, the United States did pursue an FTA with South Korea, which also had sensitive agricultural issues but was willing to address them within the context of an FTA. Although agriculture is also a sensitive issue with China, the country also recently acceded to the WTO (December 2001), is still implementing those commitments, and has been in transition to a more market-based economy. Similarly, Taiwan has recently acceded to the WTO.

After the top few non-FTA trade partners, remaining trade partners each account for about 1 percent or less of U.S. trade.[45] Since most of the smaller non-FTA trade partners are WTO members, successful conclusion of the WTO Doha Round would still provide market liberalization. However, a Doha agreement would be less likely to completely eliminate trade barriers; FTAs provide much deeper liberalization for individual countries by eliminating trade barriers between the United States and its FTA partners. Nevertheless, various studies conclude that a Doha agreement, even though unlikely to eliminate all trade barriers, would still have a much larger impact on global—and overall U.S.—trade than eliminating all trade barriers with small non-FTA partners.

Comparing countries pursued under TPA with those not pursued shows some differences in the U.S. trade and investment relationship between these two groups.[46] Overall, the U.S. tends to (1) maintain more balanced trade with TPA countries, (2) export relatively more manufactured goods (compared with services and agriculture), and (3) have relatively faster investment growth with TPA countries, particularly in countries with FTAs in effect. While these differences do not necessarily indicate the reasons countries were chosen to be pursued, they do provide useful context for the overall U.S. economic relationships with these countries as those relationships get deepened. Appendix IV discusses these differences in more detail.

Chapter 6

USTR Consulted Extensively with Congressional Staff, but Staff Have Mixed Views about Having a Meaningful Opportunity for Input

Although USTR consulted frequently with Congress, some congressional staff said that both the nature of the consultations and issues such as timing of the consultations limited congressional input into FTAs. TPA requires consultations with Congress before, during, and after FTA negotiations,[47] and records indicate consultations were extensive, particularly with the primary trade committees. The preponderance of congressional staff we interviewed viewed the consultation process as generally a good conduit for information flow from USTR. While slightly less than half of the staff we interviewed were satisfied with the quality of consultations, slightly more than half believed that the consultations did not provide the opportunity for meaningful input or influence into trade negotiations. An important element of this perception for many of these staff, particularly staff not on the trade or agriculture committees, was their view that the timing of the consultation meetings did not give them sufficient time to provide meaningful input to the negotiations. Several staff also cited situations where USTR had not fully informed them of important changes in the draft text under negotiation. Process issues of concern included the role and function of COG, selection of FTA partners, use of mock markup and the lack of a mock conference, the need to get Congress to focus on trade agreements earlier in the process, the need for additional technical information, access to USTR's secure Web site, and the importance of congressional staff working on FTAs obtaining security clearances to facilitate the consultation process.

TPA REQUIRES SIGNIFICANT CONSULTATION WITH CONGRESS

In addition to requiring the President to consult with Congress before, during, and after trade agreement negotiations, TPA also established the Congressional Oversight Group, known as COG.[48] COG is to be consulted at key points in trade negotiations, and its members are accredited as official advisors to the U.S. negotiating delegation. COG was designed to consult with and provide advice to USTR regarding the formulation of specific objectives, negotiating strategies and positions, development of trade agreements, and compliance and enforcement of negotiated commitments. Its meetings were with the U.S. Trade Representative. COG's members were the Chairs and Ranking Minority Members of the Senate Finance and House Ways and Means Committees plus two majority and one minority Member from each. In addition, membership was extended to the Chair and Ranking Minority Member of each House and Senate committee that had jurisdiction over issues affected by the negotiations, including agriculture and fisheries, which were specifically designated by TPA for consultations.

TPA also contained a detailed time line for required consultations, as shown in figure 3.

Before beginning trade negotiations, the President must[49]:

- notify Congress in writing of an intention to commence negotiations at least 90 days before initiating negotiations;
- consult, before, and after the submission of the notice, with the House Ways and Means Committee, the Senate Finance Committee, other relevant committees, and COG; and
- conduct consultations with Congress regarding agriculture, import sensitive agricultural products, the fishing industry, and textiles. During negotiations, or before entering into (signing) trade agreements, the President must[50]:
- consult with the House Ways and Means, Senate Finance, other committees with jurisdiction over legislation involving matters affected by the trade agreement, and COG, with respect to the nature of the agreement, how it achieves congressional objectives set forth in TPA, and the effect the agreement may have on existing laws;
- report to the House Ways and Means and Senate Finance committees on any changes to U.S. trade remedy laws that an agreement would require at least 180 days before entering into the agreement;[51]

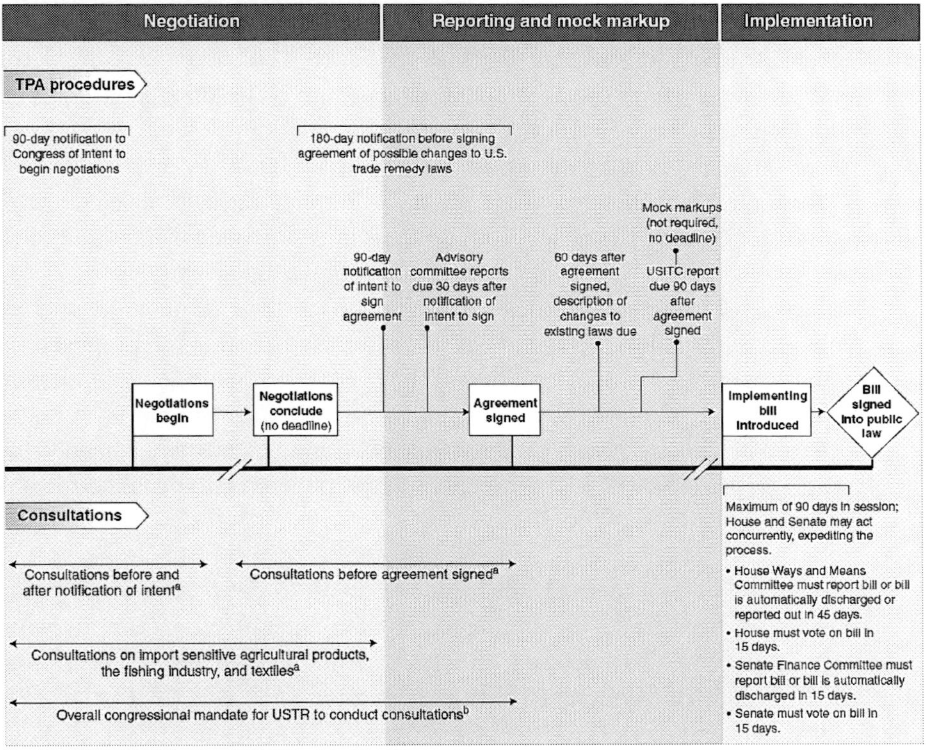

Source: GAO.

[a]TPA mandated specific consultations at a particular stage of the negotiations or related to particular industries.

[b]TPA also had an overall mandate for ongoing USTR consultations with Congress: "In the course of negotiations conducted under this title, the United States Trade Representative shall consult closely and on a timely basis with, and keep fully apprised of the negotiations, the Congressional Oversight Group convened under section 2107 and all committees of the House of Representatives and the Senate with jurisdiction over laws that would be affected by a trade agreement resulting from the negotiations." (Trade Act of 2002 Section 2102(d)(1).)

Figure 3. Congressional Time Line for Consultations under TPA.

- notify Congress of intent to enter into the agreement at least 90 days before doing so;
- submit private sector advisory committee reports to Congress within 30 days of notifying Congress of intent to enter into an agreement; and
- provide the ITC, at least 90 days before entering into the agreement, with the details of the agreement and request that ITC conduct an assessment of the likely economic impact of the agreement; the ITC must then present this assessment to the President and Congress no later than 90

days after the President enters into the agreement. There are also consultation requirements for the period between when the President signs the agreement and when the implementing legislation is voted upon in Congress. In order for the agreement to enter into force, the President must do the following during this period[52]:

- submit to the Congress, within 60 days after entering into the agreement, a description of the changes to existing laws that would be required to bring the United States into compliance with the agreement; and
- submit to Congress the final legal text of the agreement, a draft of an implementing bill, a statement of administrative action proposed to implement the trade agreement, and other supporting information, including a statement describing how the agreement makes progress in achieving goals set by Congress in TPA and a statement on how the agreement serves U.S. commercial interests; there is no deadline for this step.

If Congress believes that the President has failed to meet these consultation requirements, it may make the implementing bill ineligible for consideration under TPA procedures by adopting a procedural disapproval resolution in both houses.[53] In addition, Congress limits trade promotion authority by making it a time-limited authority.[54] The most recent grant of TPA expired July 1, 2007. It could have expired 2 years earlier had Congress passed a resolution that was introduced to disapprove of its extension. Finally, TPA includes language stating that TPA procedures are rules and that Congress retains the right of either house to change the rules.[55] In combination with the need to secure congressional approval of each agreement, these conditions all help ensure Congress's influence over agreements.

USTR HAS CONSULTED FREQUENTLY WITH CONGRESS

USTR had held frequent consultation meetings with Congress on FTA-related issues, as well as other topics. USTR consulted with Congress 1,605 times on FTA-related issues between the date TPA was signed into law on August 6, 2002, and the cutoff date for our analysis, April 20, 2007, according to a copy of USTR's consultation log. Of these consultations, 1,289 were related to specific FTAs, and 316 were related to general FTA issues, such as investment provisions or agriculture issues.[56] Consultations were primarily in-person meetings with the trade and agriculture committees but also included conference calls, particularly with the other committees of jurisdiction.

Most USTR consultations (83 percent) were with staff of congressional committees with jurisdiction over trade issues. USTR met 459 times with the Senate Finance Committee and 454 times with the House Ways and Means Committee. (See figure 4.) It met 153 times with the House Agriculture Committee and 152 times with the Senate Agriculture, Nutrition, and Forestry Committee. Thus, about two-thirds of USTR's consultations were with these four committees. USTR also met with the other committees that had jurisdiction over the following:

- *Fisheries*–Senate Commerce, Science and Transportation and House Natural Resources;
- *Intellectual property, competition, and immigration*–House and Senate Judiciary;
- *Financial services*–House Financial Services and Senate Banking, Housing, and Urban Affairs;
- *Telecommunications*–House Energy and Commerce and Senate Commerce, Science and Transportation; and
- *Government procurement*–House Oversight and Government Reform and Senate Homeland Security and Governmental Affairs.

In addition to these meetings, 163, or 9 percent, of meetings were with individual Senators and Representatives, and 3 percent were with staff of individual Senators and Representatives. Another 2 percent of meetings were with other committees, caucuses, or congressional groups. COG met as a body nine times, constituting less than 1 percent of meetings. USTR also met with the Senate Foreign Relations Committee seven times and the House International Relations Committee four times on matters related to FTAs.

A USTR official told us that the majority of meetings were open to both majority and minority committee staff, as well as to legislative assistants of Members of Congress on the committees. This is consistent with GAO analysis of the USTR logs, which showed that 148, or 11 percent, of the 1,329 meetings with staff of committees of jurisdiction were with majority members only, and 6 percent were with minority members only.[57] This was also confirmed in our interviews with congressional staff.

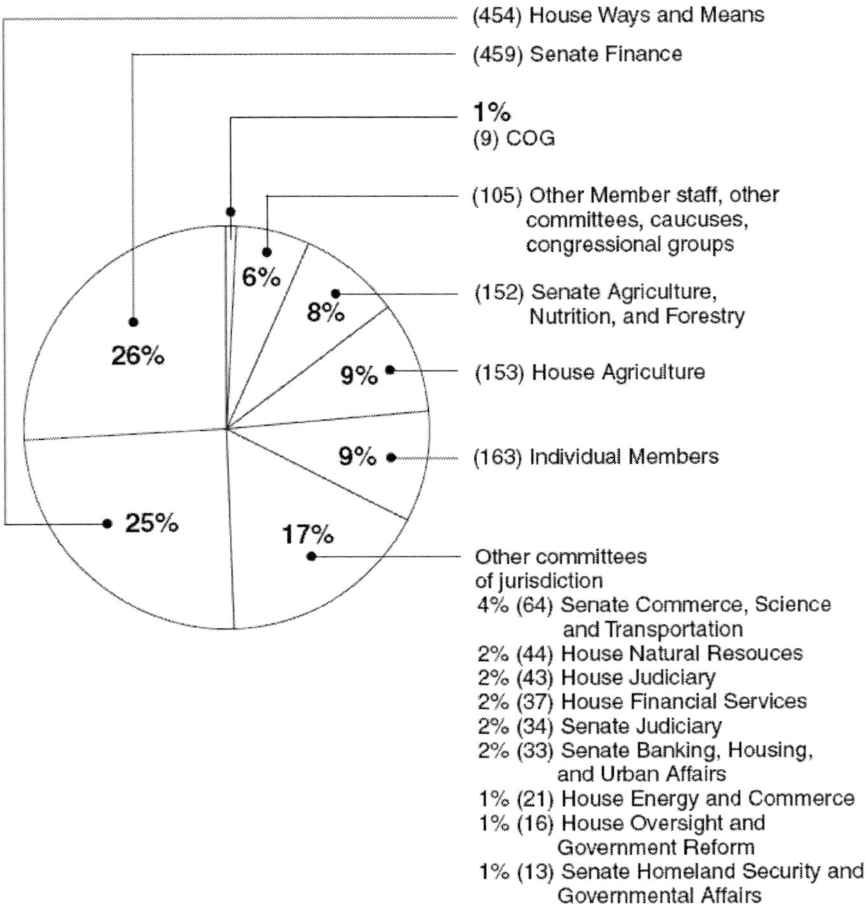

Source: GAO.

Note: Numbers total greater than 1,605 because some meetings included multiple committees or congressional entities.

Figure 4. USTR Consultations with Congress.

Current and former USTR officials told us that, for each FTA, they met with Congress throughout the process of negotiating and implementing the agreement. This was generally confirmed in our interviews with congressional staff. These officials said they met with Congress before negotiations began, before each negotiating round (with more congressional meetings in the later rounds of each FTA), before signing agreements, during congressional consideration of the FTA implementing legislation, and during FTA implementation. They said that they provided the classified negotiating text to the staff with security clearances on the trade and agriculture committees in advance of each round and discussed it at the consultation meetings. These officials said there was ample opportunity for committee staff to provide input during the negotiations and that they valued the insights they gained as to what was important to the committees. USTR officials said that they had never turned down a request for a briefing and believed that they had fully consulted with Congress. One former negotiator said that they could not conceive of a way that USTR could do more consultations than it does now and that consultations were both extensive and substantive.

As required by TPA,[58] USTR developed guidelines for COG in consultation with Congress that established notice, consultation, and reporting requirements for agreements negotiated under TPA. USTR officials said that in developing these guidelines they consulted with the Senate Finance and House Ways and Means Committees and got their input. These guidelines provide that, in the course of negotiations, USTR will consult "closely and on a timely basis" with COG and all House and Senate committees with jurisdiction over laws that would be affected by an agreement.

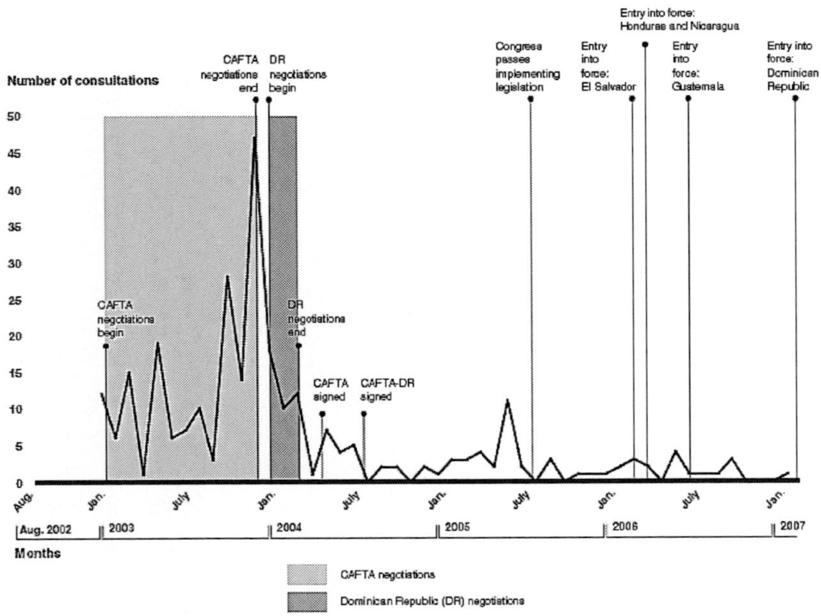

Source: GAO analysis of USTR data.

Figure 5. USTR Congressional Consultations on CAFTA-DR.

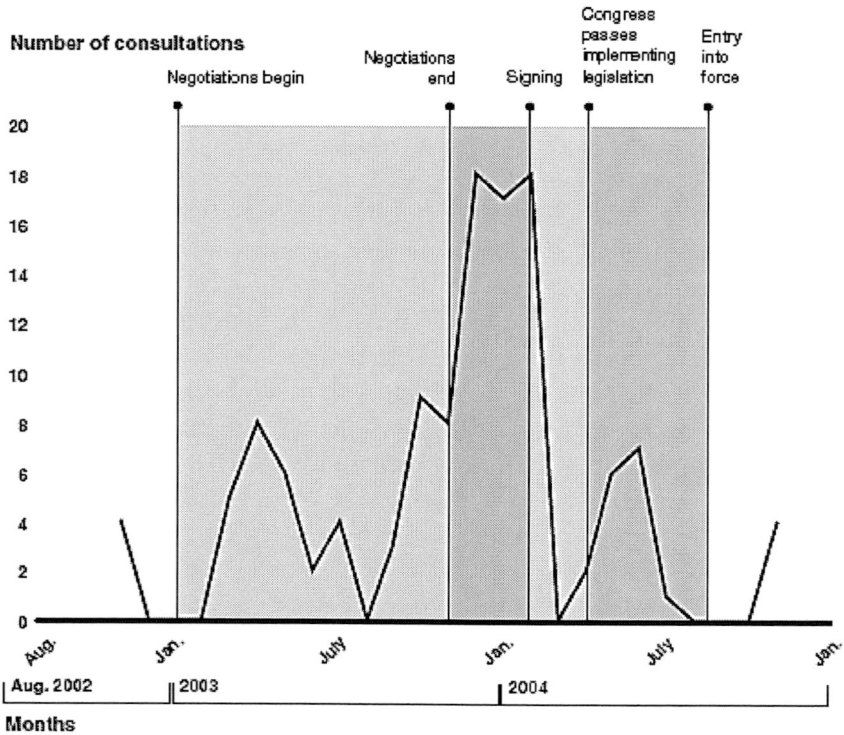

Source: GAO analysis of USTR data.

Figure 6. USTR Congressional Consultations on Australia FTA.

To verify that consultations occurred before, during, and after negotiations, we analyzed consultation patterns for two agreements. Figures 5 and 6 show the number of USTR consultations with Congress on CAFTA-DR and on the Australia FTA over time in relation to key points in the negotiation and implementation process.

We also analyzed the total number of congressional consultations on FTA-specific and FTA-related topics and found they varied over time. (See figure 7.) There were more consultations when more FTAs were under negotiation at the same time. There were also more consultations in the 1 ½ years after TPA passed in 2002, when model text for each of the 16 standard FTA chapters was being developed.

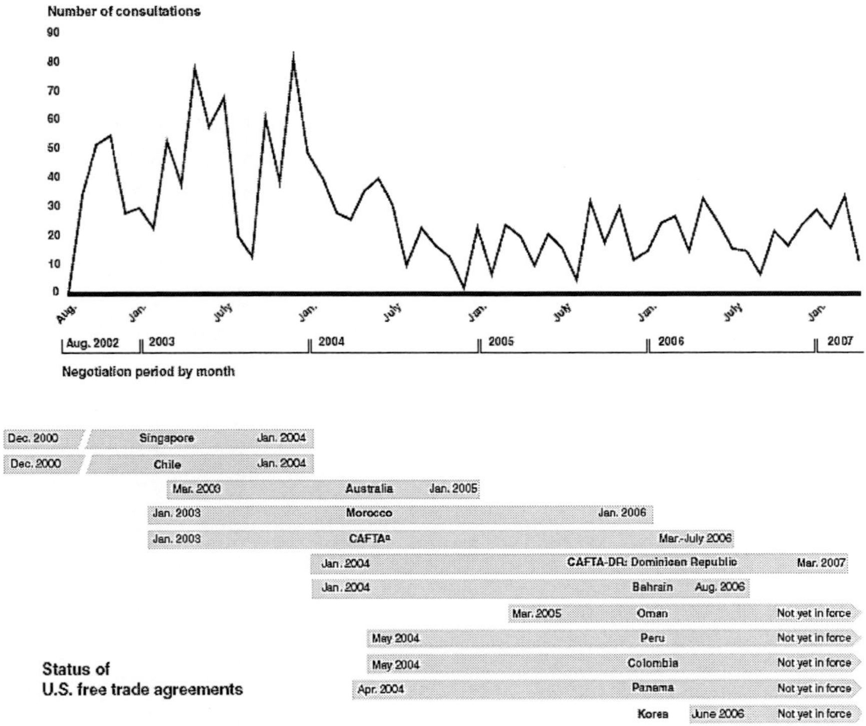

Source: GAO analysis of USTR data.

Note: The dates shown for the status of FTAs are the dates the negotiations were launched and entered into force. The Oman FTA has been approved but has not yet been implemented. The implementing legislation for the FTAs with Peru, Colombia, Panama, and South Korea have not yet been approved.

[a] Costa Rica approved the agreement by referendum on Oct. 7, 2007; domestic legal procedures have not yet concluded.

Figure 7. USTR Congressional Consultations on All FTA-Specific and FTA-Related Topics, August 6, 2002, to April 20, 2007, with Chronology and Status of FTA Negotiations.

Some Congressional Staff Noted Improvements that Could Be Made to Content and Process of Consultations

Current and former congressional committee staff[59] on key committees with jurisdiction over matters covered by FTAs[60] provided us with their views[61] on a range of issues related to the FTA consultations. These issues included the nature and extent of consultation meetings, as well as how well they met their expectations and needs.

Consultations Weekly with Trade Committees, Less Frequently with Others

From August 2002 to April 2007, the trade committees (Senate Finance and House Ways and Means) generally had weekly consultation meetings with USTR officials that often lasted an hour to an hour-and-a-half. Sometimes two or even three such meetings were held back to back on the various FTAs being negotiated. Typically, the USTR lead negotiator[62] and members of the FTA negotiating team would meet in person with the committee. Occasionally, the USTR staff were joined by staff from other agencies, such as the Departments of Agriculture or Commerce. Generally, these meetings were bipartisan, with both majority and minority professional committee staff invited, as well as the responsible legislative assistants of the Senators or Representatives that were members of the committee.[63]

Trade committee staff said that most consultation meetings were held in person. Some were conducted through a conference call, which was usually shorter. Generally, there were more conference calls at the end of the negotiations, when the USTR negotiators were more pressed for time or were overseas at negotiating sessions and calling back to update the committee staff on progress. Some of the trade committee staff we interviewed commented that in-person meetings were much more useful, although they understood the need for conference calls.

The trade committee staff we spoke with said that consultations generally took place before and after each negotiating round. Before each round, USTR provided the confidential text that it was going to table in the negotiations with the FTA partner country. Staff with security clearances had access to this text; staff without clearances received more general information.[64] After each negotiating round, USTR updated congressional staff on the issues that had been raised, the progress made, and what they thought the next round would bring.

The agriculture committees had consultation meetings with USTR approximately every 2 weeks, with the Department of Agriculture generally accompanying the USTR negotiators, according to a committee staff person. Otherwise, the descriptions of the consultation meetings were mostly similar to those of the trade committee staff. In contrast, the other committees of jurisdiction generally had a much more limited experience with consultation meetings than the trade and agriculture committees, which are the main committees of jurisdiction regarding FTA issues. Generally, the issues involved in the FTA negotiations were not priority issues for these committees, and many of them had a much more limited understanding of the proceedings. Most did not have clearances and received more general descriptions of provisions that would be negotiated, since they were not cleared to receive actual negotiating text.

The number of consultation meetings for these committees was substantially less than for the trade and agriculture committees and varied from once a month to once for each FTA.

Consultations Generally Praised for Providing High-Quality Information but Satisfaction with Input and Influence Mixed

Almost all of the committee staff we interviewed said that USTR provided high-quality information that provided them with insight into the progress of the negotiations. In this respect, they met the expectations of these congressional staff for information related to the FTA negotiations. These staff felt that the briefings were very well done. They also praised USTR's willingness to answer questions and follow up on particular issues of interest. The general view was that USTR was very responsive in answering questions and providing follow-up information.

In terms of satisfaction that the consultation meetings provided an opportunity for input or influence on the trade negotiations, however, the committee staff we interviewed were fairly evenly divided.[65] Slightly less than half of the congressional staff we interviewed felt that the consultation meetings had met their expectations in this respect as well. They were satisfied that they had been fully briefed, and the USTR negotiators had listened to their views. They indicated that they knew that USTR could not always obtain the results their committee or their Member of Congress wanted, but felt that their views had been taken into consideration. However, slightly more than half of the congressional committee staff with whom we spoke felt that they did not have any real input or influence on the trade negotiations. For these staff, USTR's consultation meetings had not met their expectations because they had not provided an opportunity for a two-way exchange of information that the staff considered a true consultation. One committee staff person appeared to reflect the views of these staff in characterizing the consultations as a good conduit for information flow from USTR, but not as a good forum for working together and developing policy jointly. Others characterized the meetings as helping them feel well-briefed, but not consulted. Among these staff, several said they felt that USTR was "checking the box" in their meetings with them. At the same time, among the staff who indicated that the consultations were more of a one-way briefing than a two-way consultation, several were on the other committees of jurisdiction and said they did not have expectations of more. They said that they were satisfied with receiving briefings because this was not a priority issue for them or because they did not expect to influence the negotiations. Overall, on this issue, the degree to which the committee staff we interviewed felt that they had input or influence on trade negotiations varied across parties. In particular, Republican staff (which was in the majority in Congress for nearly all of the TPA period) generally had more positive views about their input and influence than Democrats.

We also found mixed views among the staff we interviewed on whether the timing of the consultations gave sufficient time for staff to provide meaningful input. Most, but not all, of the staff of the trade and agriculture committees said the timeliness of consultations was good.[66] However, staff from the other committees of jurisdiction often said that the consultations were not timely and cited this as a reason that they felt briefed rather than consulted. They said that they generally weren't briefed and given information until the last business day before the negotiators were leaving for the next round. This did not give them enough time to fully consider the information, consult with their committee or Member to develop a response, and give feedback that USTR would have time to consider. These staff felt strongly that one way to achieve more meaningful congressional input was to allow more time for feedback by having earlier consultations and by providing them with text or other information in a more timely manner. In addition, staff of one of the primary committees of jurisdiction complained of last-minute consultations on some of the more controversial issues. While they understood that the interagency process took time and that USTR was moving as quickly as possible, they felt that if congressional consultation was meant to be meaningful, USTR could either build in the time needed for congressional consultation or delay tabling the controversial text at the next negotiating round to allow time for congressional input.

Among the committee staff who had expressed satisfaction with the consultation meetings, several noted that the style of the briefer was important. In some cases, the briefers tended to keep the briefing short and let committee staff ask questions. The staff we spoke with said that if they asked a question, the briefers would answer it fully. But, if staffers didn't know what to ask, they were at a disadvantage in obtaining pertinent information. They said that most staff depended on the briefers to let them know about issues of concern. This was very important to them. It was much more helpful when the briefers provided the context and alerted them to any changes in the text or any areas of concern developing in the negotiations.

Several other committee staff, who were dissatisfied with the consultations, expressed a much more negative view about briefers' willingness to share information. While they agreed that the information USTR provided was generally of good quality, they said there were instances when, in their opinion,

USTR deliberately did not offer information on changes to the negotiated text that would be of concern to staffers, unless they asked specific questions, which they often did not know to ask. One committee staff said that this had been the case, for example, with the U.S.-Korea FTA, in which significant changes had been made to the investment chapter. Although the committee staff had received the amended text, USTR did not mention that changes had been made to a sensitive provision in the Expropriation Annex, which the committee staff said was extremely controversial—to the point that the language in the text had been carefully worked out in the 2001-2002 time period and then never touched again. The staff person said that this text was considered to be "set in stone," and any change to it clearly merited mention by USTR. With the press of business during consideration of the U.S.-Korea FTA, the committee staff had not realized that it had been changed, and they didn't learn about it until they were alerted by the private sector. The committee staff who were dissatisfied with the consultations also said that there had been instances when it appeared USTR had withheld information. For example, several committee staff mentioned that a controversy related to the Australia FTA pharmaceuticals benefits scheme resulted from USTR withholding information. Again, committee staff found out about the controversial provisions from the private sector when the text was made public. In another example, some committee staff said that USTR had not adequately briefed Judiciary Committee staff on the H1-B visas issue with the Chile and Singapore FTAs. While there was disagreement among the staff who commented on this as to whether USTR had adequately briefed the staff or withheld critical information, a lack of clarity in the consultations did result in the Judiciary Committee being highly upset about this issue. (As a result of the Judiciary Committee's views, USTR significantly modified its objectives regarding immigration. Subsequent agreements have either included a side letter stating that the agreement has no effect on U.S. immigration law or policy or, in more recent agreements, this type of provision has been included in the text of the agreement.) These staff felt strongly that in order for the consultation process to work, Members of Congress and committee staff need to know that USTR will always make a good faith effort to tell them when substantive changes to the model text have been made in the negotiations. In FTAs, specific details that are negotiated are critical to the outcome.

Many Staff Cite Shortcomings in Consultation Process

Congressional staff also expressed concerns about the consultation process, including the usefulness of COG, the congressional role in FTA partner selection, the role of mock markup, the importance of earlier congressional focus on FTA negotiations, the need for greater access to technical information, and problems with access to USTR's secure website. Most of these issues focused more on internal congressional matters than on USTR. In addition, USTR also stressed the importance of congressional staff working on FTAs to obtain security clearances to facilitate the consultation process.

COG Generally Not Seen as Successful

COG was a new mechanism under TPA intended to draw Members of Congress into the consultation process, particularly members from nontrade committees, and to provide them with a private and confidential opportunity to have a consultative and advisory role in trade policy, according to a committee staff person familiar with its creation. The staff person went on to state that COG was also meant to provide greater transparency and inclusiveness to the trade policy consultation process. After it was launched in September 2002, COG was convened only nine times before TPA lapsed in July 2007, according to the USTR consultation log. COG's record drew mixed reviews. Some trade committee staff had a positive view of COG, saying that it had been a useful forum for input on FTAs, including FTA selection, or that it was worthwhile because it had provided a mechanism for transparency. However, most trade and agriculture committee staff said it had been of limited usefulness and had not functioned well. These staff said that COG was not well attended, particularly after the first few years. While the trade committee members continued to attend regularly, few others did. Some trade committee staff said that the separate committee executive sessions with their Members were more useful than COG. Most staff outside of the trade and agriculture committees with whom we spoke were unfamiliar with COG or unaware it existed; those staff who were familiar with COG did not find it to be useful.

USTR officials and committee staff noted that it was difficult to schedule meetings around the busy schedules of Members of Congress. One committee staff said that it had been difficult to schedule attendance by the Member because of short notice for the COG meetings, pointing out that it would be helpful if COG meetings were put on a regular schedule. Two committee staff said a limitation of COG was the requirement that staff could only attend with their Member, so they could not cover meetings the Member could not attend. Another committee staff said that COG meetings should not be scheduled solely at the discretion of the majority staff but also by the minority in order to protect minority rights. Several committee staff described the COG meetings as formalities, particularly as time went on. One staff of a Member on a trade committee, but not on the COG, said that they had resented being excluded from this trade policy-making forum.

FTA Partner Selection Concerns Due to Lack of Commercial Significance

Most congressional staff we interviewed who had a view on this issue felt that their committee did not have any meaningful input into the selection of FTA partner countries. However, there was substantially more awareness and concern about this issue among the trade and agriculture committee staff than among staff of other committees of jurisdiction.[67]

Among those concerned about partner selection, the primary concern seemed to be that so many smaller trading partners were being selected for FTA negotiations, rather than larger trading partners with greater commercial and economic significance. One committee staff commented that, increasingly, every congressional vote for an FTA was a difficult vote that involved using up significant political capital. While Members supporting free trade had no problem in principle with negotiating FTAs with smaller countries for foreign policy or other reasons, if Members were going to be expending significant political capital, they wanted it to at least be economically and commercially beneficial. Another committee staff said that the selection of FTA partners and dialogue about it with Congress should be more transparent and that the reasoning behind the choices of FTA partners and the complicating factors should be openly discussed.

Some staff said that in TPA the role of input into FTA partner selection had been given to COG, rather than to committee staff. Although this role was informal, some committee staff and USTR officials said that USTR took COG's advice on selection seriously and that some potential partners supported by COG had been pursued by USTR. They cited the U.S.-Korea FTA as an example.

A few committee staff favored restoring the gatekeeper provision,[68] which was part of prior fast track legislation but was dropped when TPA was passed in 2002. The gatekeeper provision had required the President to notify Congress and give it an opportunity to disapprove launching of negotiations with a particular partner.[69] These staff felt that restoring it might be beneficial in terms of potentially generating greater buy-in to the FTAs selected for negotiation. Generally, only trade committee staff were aware of the gatekeeper provision. Those opposed did not see any value in it given COG's role in discussing potential FTA partners. The former USTR negotiators with whom we discussed this issue also opposed it. They were particularly concerned about the potential effects of any requirement for an affirmative vote for launching FTA negotiations with a trade partner country because it would mean that Congress would have to vote twice for each FTA and it would force a vote before anyone knew what the actual benefits from the FTA would be.

Mock Markup Considered Important, but Mock Conference Controversial

Most trade and agriculture staff we interviewed were familiar with the mock markup process—the informal committee process to "mark up" or amend the draft implementing bills for FTAs.[70] Most trade staff said that it was an important part of the consultations process for TPA.[71] Committee mock markups are generally the only opportunity Congress has to offer amendments to the proposed FTA implementing bill. However, while some were concerned that the mock mark-up process had not been used effectively, others were concerned that it could be misused in order to delay consideration of FTAs or to introduce inappropriate last-minute provisions that should have been addressed during the negotiations.

Some also expressed concern that the trade committees had not scheduled mock conferences when the House and Senate had adopted differing mock amendments. They said that a mock conference was an important part of the consultation process. Some of these staff cited the case of CAFTA when the House and Senate versions of the draft implementing bills differed because the Senate Finance Committee and the House Ways and Means Committee had recommended different mock amendments. They said the two committees did not hold a mock conference and the administration chose the version it preferred, the House version, ignoring the Senate Finance Committee amendments. Other staffers said that complex multilateral negotiations like those of the WTO would need a mock conference, but that FTAs were simpler and a mock conference was often unnecessary and time consuming.

Earlier Congressional Focus on FTA Negotiations Seen as Important

Some committee staff felt that an inherent problem with the consultation process was that Congress tended to focus on the FTAs at the end of the negotiations, when the deal was essentially done, and it was difficult (if not impossible) to change the terms of the agreement. They said that this resulted from the congressional culture of waiting until an issue was fully developed and likely to become law before focusing on it. In contrast, they said that trade negotiations particularly require congressional attention throughout the process. For consultations to be meaningful and most effective, they felt that it would be important to find ways through the consultation process to facilitate Congress focusing earlier on the FTAs. This was particularly critical given the nature of fast track provisions, in which the final agreement comes to Congress for an up-or-down vote with no amendments.

USTR officials, including some former lead negotiators who we interviewed, also said that earlier attention by Congress was important. Some of them expressed frustration that they would hold frequent consultation meetings, but that many committee staff would not attend, or would not actively engage. Then, at the end of the process, when the negotiations were finalized, they would start to focus and ask questions and want changes. This was very ineffective—sometimes USTR was able to get changes, but often it was no longer possible to modify something that could have been changed earlier in the negotiations.

Greater Access to Technical Expertise and Information Desired

Another issue raised by several congressional staff was the need for greater access to technical information on an ongoing basis. These staff said that although committee staff on the trade and agricultural committees are knowledgeable about their fields, trade negotiations are today too broad and complex for any one staff member to fully understand all of the implications. One trade staff told us that staff on the other committees of jurisdiction are at a disadvantage because trade is not their primary issue, and they don't have time to follow it. Having access to expert staff, such as through a congressional trade office, would be very helpful, according to one committee staff. Another committee staff opposed what they feared might be creation of an additional bureaucracy with a new trade office and instead said that GAO could serve this role.

In principle, the formal private sector trade advisors could help fill this void. However, committee staff said that they did not have contact with them during the FTA negotiations. One staff said that they used to be invited to trade advisory committee meetings, but no longer. Although the trade advisory committees provide extensive technical information to Congress in their required reports on each FTA at the end of the process, committee staff did not have access to their substantial knowledge base during the negotiations.

A related issue raised by a few staff on some of the nontrade committees of jurisdiction was that trade negotiations involve a great deal of specialized terminology and information. Staff of one committee said that sometimes they found it difficult to fully understand the briefings because the negotiators used so much jargon. They said that it would be helpful if USTR developed a primer describing the typical evolution of the trade negotiations process and providing a glossary of trade terms. Other ideas included USTR providing an overview on upcoming issues at the start of the year, giving more of an overview on FTAs early on, and describing in some detail FTAs at their conclusion.

Problems with Access to Secure USTR Web Site Limits Information Availability

An issue raised by many of the trade and agriculture committee staff that we interviewed was access to USTR's secure Web site on which it posts the negotiating text for FTAs, as well as other information. The Senate staff said that this was more a matter related to internal congressional security issues than to USTR. Until this year, the Senate committee staff that have access to the classified negotiating texts said they received hard copy information because the Senate was unable to resolve security concerns to allow electronic access. When USTR sent a hard copy to the Office of Senate Security, it took the office a day to log it in and notify staff of its availability. Then staff had to make an appointment to go to a secure room in the Capitol in order to read these documents. The result was that they had a significantly smaller window of time to access the documents than if they had been immediately available electronically. Staffers said that recently a computer in a Senate office building had been made available for this purpose. While this was an improvement, they would prefer to have access in their own offices, or at least their own buildings. On the House side, committee staff did not have any electronic access to USTR's secure Web site, as of the end of August 2007. However, several committee staff said that access was being planned and would greatly improve timely staff access to negotiating information.

USTR officials said that they would welcome expansion of congressional access to USTR's secure Web site. They also said that an important related issue is whether congressional staff working on FTAs under negotiation had security clearances. USTR officials felt strongly that if more congressional staff obtained security clearances, it would greatly facilitate the consultation process, both in terms of access to information and timeliness of information.

Chapter 7

CONSULTATIONS AFFORD TRADE ADVISORY COMMITTEES ACCESS, BUT PROCESS ISSUES IMPEDE EFFECTIVE PROVISION OF ADVICE

The trade advisory committee chairs we contacted said that USTR and the managing executive branch agencies consulted with their committees on a fairly regular basis, providing access to administration officials, but process issues made it difficult for some committees to function effectively. In addition to consultations with Congress, the administration is required to consult with private sector advisory committees and with the public at large[72] to get a sense of their views. We spoke with 16 chairs of the relevant 27 trade advisory committees, as well as five additional committee members.[73] They reported that consultations were generally extensive in number. The chairs and members, however, had mixed reactions as to whether the nature of the consultations, quality of information provided, and feedback received were satisfactory. Furthermore, process issues such as reporting time frames, committee composition, and chartering and appointment sometimes impeded advisory committees' ability to provide advice on trade negotiations.

CONSULTATIONS WITH TRADE ADVISORY COMMITTEES WERE GENERALLY EXTENSIVE

Four agencies, led by USTR, administer the three-tiered trade advisory committee system. (See figure 8.) USTR directly administers the first tier overall policy committee, the President's Advisory Committee for Trade Policy and

Negotiations (ACTPN), and three of the second tier general policy committees, the Trade Advisory Committee on Africa (TACA),[74] the Intergovernmental Policy Advisory Committee (IGPAC), and the Trade and Environment Policy Advisory Committee (TEPAC), for which the Environmental Protection Agency also plays a supporting role. The Department of Labor coadministers the second tier Labor Advisory Committee (LAC) and the Department of Agriculture coadministers the second tier Agricultural Policy Advisory Committee (APAC). The Department of Agriculture also coadministers the third tier Agricultural Technical Advisory Committees (ATACs), while the Department of Commerce coadministers the third tier Industry Trade Advisory Committees (ITACs). Ultimately, member appointments to the committees have to be cleared by both the Secretary of the managing agency and the U.S. Trade Representative, as they are the appointing officials.

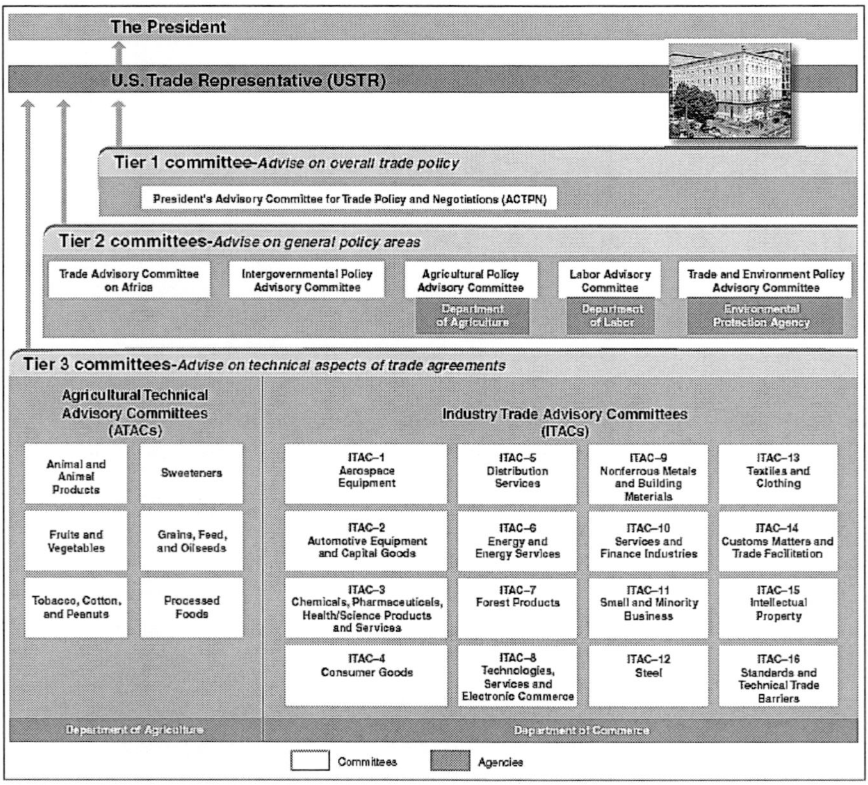

Sources: GAO and USTR.

Figure 8. Trade Advisory Committee System.

USTR and the relevant executive branch agencies consulted with the first and third tier advisory committees on a fairly regular basis. The first and third tier chairs we contacted generally felt that these consultations provided the committees with important access to the administration and ongoing negotiations. From fiscal year 2002 through May of fiscal year 2007, USTR met with the 16 ITACs[75] a total of 729 times. From fiscal year 2002 through fiscal year 2006, USTR met with the six ATACs a total of 92 times. Most of these meetings were in person, although conference calls were sometimes held for fast-moving issues or during the 30-day time frame for report writing. In addition, USTR established a monthly conference call for all trade advisory committee chairs, beginning in late 2002.

The number of consultations with USTR was more limited at the second tier policy committee level. Although USTR has met fairly regularly with APAC and TEPAC over the past 5 years, the LAC had no meetings for over 2 years from September 2003 to November 2005. Furthermore, IGPAC did not have an in-person consultation with USTR from July 2005 to September 2007. In late 2006, USTR instituted a monthly conference call for IGPAC, together with state points of contact.[76] Agency officials said this was done to broaden outreach to the states and increase the frequency of interaction with USTR without travel costs. The officials added that they have also convened additional IGPAC conference call meetings, as needed on particular issues. LAC and TEPAC (as well as ACTPN) have liaison groups that meet more often. For example, the TEPAC liaison group tries to meet every 4 to 6 weeks. According to members from these committees, liaison meetings are at the staff level and are usually fairly technical, whereas the principals' meetings tend to look at broader, political issues.

Committees Had Mixed Reactions to Nature of Consultations

Slightly over half of the committee chairs we interviewed felt that their expectations of the consultation process were met, but overall views on the opportunity to provide meaningful input varied. For example, one third tier chair said that his expectations were met since the process works well to facilitate access between negotiators and private sector representatives, and the administration seems to take consultations seriously. The second tier committees in particular, however, stated that their advice and opinions were not considered. A few of the third tier committees concurred. Those who said their expectations were not met told us their committees were not being used properly. According to a few of these chairs, while the administration has consultation meetings with them, they are more to "check off the box" than to engage in meaningful dialogue. The chairs feel that the administration tells them what has already been decided upon instead of soliciting their advice. Furthermore, two ITAC chairs told us that it is more effective to use venues other than the advisory committee system to provide meaningful input. For example, one chair said that a coalition of industry-related companies outside of the ITAC is the major venue for consultations with the administration for that industry. The chair told us that the ITAC advisory process tends to be at the end of negotiations and is not as significant as it should be. At the same time, the chair felt the ITAC did play a role in the consultation process. Although it could not consult at the highly technical level that the coalition could, it was able to consult on the broad direction of U.S. trade policy for that industry. USTR officials told us that the fact that the advice of any particular advisory committee may not be reflected in a trade agreement does not mean that the advice was not carefully considered. USTR emphasized that it does consider advice from its advisory committees in formulating U.S. trade policy. At the same time, however, USTR also acknowledged that for some contentious issues, the advice is not in line with long-standing U.S. policy or congressional guidance set out in TPA. In those instances, USTR told us they are very limited in what they can do in response to advisory committee advice. This appears to be particularly problematic for second tier policy advisory committees. For example, the strength and reach of FTA investment provisions and dispute settlement mechanisms have long been a concern of both IGPAC and TEPAC. LAC, meanwhile, has criticized the worker rights standards and dispute settlement mechanisms in FTAs as insufficient.

Overall, the first tier and most of the third tier committee chairs we interviewed felt that the information USTR provided was of high quality and detail, providing a mixture of publicly available information and more proprietary, confidential information. Most of the second tier policy committee and a few third tier technical committee chairs in our selection, however, were not satisfied with the quality of information presented during consultations and felt that it was no better than information available to the general public. Of those committees, one chair felt USTR was constantly holding back information, and the committee learned something new only every seventh or eighth meeting. Another chair expressed frustration at trying to get information as negotiations were in progress, saying that USTR was reluctant to state what the other country was proposing. Two of the chairs who were dissatisfied went on to say that although most of the information presented is available publicly, having access to administration officials was valuable. Several other committee chairs also emphasized the value they place on having access to the administration through the advisory committee process.

Approximately half of the advisory committee chairs with whom we spoke felt that the administration was responsive to their advice and provided feedback, whether or not their advice was incorporated into the agreement. The first tier and over half of the third tier committee chairs feel there is an adequate opportunity for dialogue and that their interests are considered. Most of the second tier and a few of the third tier committee chairs, however, expressed dissatisfaction with the feedback from USTR. They expressed their perception that USTR is either biased against their committee or that by being asked to comment on completed deals, their opinions are not truly valued or taken into consideration. Two chairs said USTR wants them to "rubber-stamp" decisions or to be "cheerleaders" for the administration. Other chairs said their committees rarely or never get feedback.

In general, the advisory committee chairs we spoke with were pleased with the numerous changes that have been made to the advisory committee system in response to GAO's 2002 report. In particular, members found the secure Web site very useful. A quarter of the chairs said that having text on the Web site sooner, or when USTR says it will be posted, would be helpful, but they agreed that the secure Web site was a valuable tool. Three-quarters of the chairs we interviewed had no complaints about the reconfiguration of the committee system to more closely align with the current U.S. economy, although chairs and members from slightly over a third of the committees we interviewed found problems with the representation of interests on their individual committees. Ten of the 16 chairs with whom we spoke did not find the monthly chairs' teleconference call useful, primarily because of a lack of detailed information; those chairs located in Washington, D.C., cited lack of new information. Furthermore, 8 of the 11 chairs we interviewed whose committees are invited to the newly instituted periodic plenary meetings[77] (ATACs and ITACs) did not find them useful. A couple of those chairs did acknowledge, however, that their out-of-town members might find them more useful and that they are a good opportunity to hear cabinet-level speakers to whom they would not routinely have access. Beyond the plenary meetings, several chairs, particularly among the ITACs, said that more interaction with other advisory committees would be useful. Currently, only three ITACs (Customs Matters and Trade Facilitation, Intellectual Property Rights, and Standards and Technical Trade Barriers) allow for members from other ITACs to sit in on meetings in a nonvoting capacity. There is also an Investment Working Group that draws from across the ITAC committees that a couple of chairs said was a helpful device.

Other Stakeholders Found Public Hearings Ineffective or Did Not Participate

Stakeholders outside of the trade advisory committee system were also provided an opportunity to express their views on the record through the public hearing process; however, they have found other methods to be more effective. The administration holds public hearings and gives the public an opportunity to submit written comments for each FTA. Anyone is free to come to these meetings and express their opinions.

We spoke with three of the former Assistant U.S. Trade Representatives who were in charge of negotiating FTAs over the past 5 years under TPA, and each said that the public hearing process was useful and gave USTR a good overall sense of what issues were important to the general public. They noted that they sometimes gained information from viewpoints not represented in the formal system and that comments were distributed to responsible officials and taken into account.

While we did not speak extensively with stakeholders that used these formal and informal avenues for input, we spoke with a few trade experts in the nongovernmental organization and academic communities that had used them or were familiar with them. The experts from the academic community admitted that although they were aware of the public hearing process, they did not participate in it. Those in the nongovernmental organization community, however, had either personally participated or their organization had, but they did not feel that their opinions were heard. Furthermore, they felt left out of the process and that industry groups had much better access. As a result, these groups said they have to go directly to Congress to express their opinions through hearings or personal contact.

Process Issues Impeded Committees' Function

Despite the frequency and quality of USTR consultations with the advisory committees, process issues such as short reporting time frames, lack of transparency in committee composition, and delays in rechartering committees and appointing members sometimes impeded committees' ability to provide trade advice.

Reporting Deadlines Are Difficult to Meet

The Trade Act of 1974 requires trade advisory committees to provide to the President, the Congress, and USTR a report detailing their advisory opinion as to (1) whether and to what extent the agreement promotes the economic interests of the United States and achieves the applicable overall and principal negotiating objectives (for first and second tier committees) and (2) whether the agreement provides for equity and reciprocity within the sector or within the functional area.[78] TPA legislation gives the advisory committees 30 days after the President notifies Congress of the intent to sign a trade agreement to submit these reports.

Approximately half of the committee chairs we interviewed said that this deadline can be difficult to meet for both technical and logistical reasons, and the committees cannot always give advice based on a thorough review. Reasons they gave include the following:

- FTAs are technical, complex documents including thousands of lines of tariffs.
- Advisory committee members are volunteers with full-time jobs and other commitments.
- Coordinating the FTA review and report within 30 days can be a challenge.
- The text is sometimes not available until several days into the 30-day period.
- Negotiations are not always finalized for all sectors at the same time, and the posting of various chapters is staggered.
- Although committee members see versions of the text as the FTA develops, the final agreed-upon text can change the implications for their particular interest significantly.

The FTA with South Korea provides the most obvious and recent example of presenting a challenge in meeting the deadline. Chairs told us the text was not available to their committees until between 7 and 14 of the 30 days had passed. Furthermore, although some issues such as rice had been agreed upon in principle between the United States and South Korea at the conclusion of the agreement and the advisors had been briefed on the results, the final text had not yet been written. According to administration officials, the FTA with South Korea was an exception, since USTR was rushing to finish negotiations before TPA expired.[79] Committee chairs told us, however, that meeting the 30-day deadline has been difficult for other FTAs as well. One of the second tier policy committee chairs, for example, noted that the committee did not have access to the agricultural sections of the final text of the Colombia FTA in time to complete the review prior to issuing a committee report. The committee therefore had to submit a pro forma letter, noting that they would provide a more detailed addendum to their report after the full text became available. A third tier committee chair told us that his committee regularly reserves the right to amend its report. USTR officials acknowledged that the time frame for report writing has been problematic for years. Furthermore, they pointed out that as USTR is actually tasked with sending all of the committee reports within 30 days to Congress, they need at least a couple of days to collect reports from the various committees, make copies, and then send them by courier.

It is also difficult for the ITC to provide in the specified time frame its statutorily required report[80] assessing the likely impact of the agreement on the U.S. economy and specific industry sectors because of delays in receiving the final agreement text. The President is required to provide the ITC with the details of the agreement, as it exists at that time, 90 days before the date on which the President enters into the agreement. The ITC has a total of 180 days from that date to hold any hearings, do its analysis, and submit its report. TPA also requires the President to update ITC on the details of the agreement during this period.[81] According to ITC officials, the deadline is often difficult to make due to last minute changes and late delivery of the final text. These officials told us that ITC sometimes does not get the full text of the agreement and all of the annexes until they are already more than halfway through the 180-day period. The ITC officials agreed with advisory committee chairs who suggested that a longer report writing window would be useful. One committee chair specifically suggested extending the window by 15 days. Commerce and USTR officials agreed that they would like to see at least 15 more days allowed for report writing.

Incorporation of Nonbusiness Interests Remains Difficult, and Committee Composition Is Not Transparent

The represented interests on trade advisory committees are not always transparent. Congress requires, through the Trade Act of 1974, that the President seek information and advice from representative elements of the private sector and the nonfederal government sector through trade advisory committees that include representatives of certain interests. For example, the first tier ACTPN is to include representatives of nonfederal governments, labor, agriculture, small business, environmental and conservation organizations, and consumer interests, among others.[82] The third tier committees are to be representative, insofar as is practicable, of all industry, labor, agricultural, or service interests in the sector or functional areas concerned.[83] After we reported in 2002 that the committee system's structure needed to be revisited, USTR and managing agencies worked with Congress in reconfiguring some of the committees. For example, the LAC membership now includes primarily union presidents to ensure that the administration receives advice from the highest levels. Furthermore, the 21 industry functional and sector committees were realigned and streamlined into 16 industry committees to more accurately reflect the current U.S. economy and trade policy needs. USTR and the other managing agencies, however, still have had difficulty incorporating nonbusiness stakeholders into the committees. For example, USTR said it has had difficulties finding labor representatives willing to serve on ACTPN, the overall policy first tier committee that is required to be broadly representative of key sectors and groups affected by trade.[84] Just under half of the committee members with whom we spoke expressed frustration with the current composition of their committees. Members who were dissatisfied with representation told us either that they felt that certain relevant viewpoints were not adequately represented or that the composition favored representation of one industry or group at the expense of another. Furthermore, some members are the sole representative of a nonbusiness interest on their committee. The nonbusiness members we spoke with told us that although their interest is now represented, they still feel isolated within their own committee. The result is the perception that their minority perspective is not influential.

Available public information makes it difficult to determine what perspective or interest a committee member represents. For example, USTR officials pointed to the charters of the committees for which USTR is the principal administrator for guidelines as to which representatives they select. The charter for TEPAC, however, simply says that members shall be from environmental interest groups, industry, agriculture, services, nonfederal governments, and consumer interests, and that they shall be broadly representative of key sectors and groups with an interest in trade and environmental policy issues. The Department of Labor's charter for LAC only says members will be selected from the U.S. labor community. In addition to charters, the Departments of Agriculture and Commerce also put out *Federal Register* notices soliciting new members. These notices stipulate that members must have expertise and knowledge of trade issues relevant to the committees and that geographic, demographic, and sector balance will be sought. Neither the charters nor the *Federal Register* notices, however, explain how the agencies actually determined which representatives they placed on committees, although these are the documents agencies continually referred us to for this information. Without reporting such an explanation, it is not transparent how agencies followed their own guidelines for member selection or met statutory representation requirements.

It is also not always transparent from the final roster which interest a particular member represents. The FACA[85] required the President to report annually on the status of advisory committees, although this requirement was terminated in 2000.[86] The General Services Administration now collects this information from the relevant executive branch agencies and posts it on the FACA database (a publicly available database on committees operating under FACA). While the Department of Commerce reports on the specific interest each committee member represents, USTR and the Departments of Agriculture and Labor do not. Instead, they list the member's occupation or affiliation. However, it is not always possible to deduce from that information a member's represented interest, as for example, several committee members are from law firms or large companies that deal with a variety of issues. Listing the name of the firm or company alone does not necessarily indicate representation of a particular interest. As a result, it is difficult to determine whether USTR is receiving the information and advice Congress intended it to obtain from these committees.

Rechartering and Appointment Processes Flawed

Weaknesses in the processes of rechartering and repopulating committees have caused significant lapses in committees' functions. Originally, FACA called for the termination of advisory committees every 2 years unless renewed or its duration is otherwise provided for by law.[87] Legislation passed in 2004 in response to our 2002 report leaves it to the discretion of the President whether or not to extend the charters of the trade advisory committees established under the Trade Act of 1974 to 4 years.[88] All of these committees, with the exception of LAC, now have 4-year charters. Department of Labor officials told us this is because of miscommunication surrounding the 2004 legislation. Charters of several committees have been allowed to lapse recently, however, resulting in committees not being able to meet for extended periods of time (up to 7 months in the case of LAC). Furthermore, the process of selecting and appointing committee members requires a number of time-consuming steps. The Department of Commerce, for example, starts the process of appointing new members approximately 9 months prior to the ITACs' charter expiration dates, to try and ensure that the work of the ITACs does not stop, and has been successful in avoiding lapses as a result. However, other agencies do not always start this process in time for committees to begin meeting once the charter is renewed. When both processes of rechartering and member appointment are delayed, it further reduces a committee's ability to give timely, official advice before the committee is terminated, and the rechartering process has to begin again. This is particularly true in the case of LAC, which still has a 2-year charter.

These periods of committees not being able to meet have occurred during important stages of the U.S. trade agenda for both bilateral agreements and the WTO. Most recently, the charters of APAC and all six of the ATACs expired on April 29, 2007. The Department of Agriculture began the process of soliciting new members on March 20. Although the committees were rechartered in late May, as of late September 2007 they had still been unable to meet because they had not yet been repopulated. A Department of Agriculture official told us that this is because key people responsible for the vetting process in the undersecretary's office have been unavailable due to travel schedules. In the interim, however, the United States signed FTAs with Panama and South Korea on June 28 and June 30, respectively. Although these committees were able to get their reports on the two FTAs to USTR just before their charters expired, they have not been able to give any official advice in the interim period, when agricultural issues—particularly rice in the FTA with South Korea—were still being negotiated. In another example, the LAC did not meet from September 2003 until November 2005.[89] Department of Labor officials indicated this was due in part to the difficulty in getting members vetted and appointed.[90] During this more than 2-year period, the United States was not only negotiating in the Doha Round of the WTO, but was also negotiating FTAs with numerous countries. The administration, however, is not required to report such lapses and the reasons behind them. The FACA database does collect data

on the length of the current charter and the number of meetings held each year. This information, however, is only reported on an annual basis, and we found several discrepancies in the data posted, including incorrect charter and meeting dates.

Chapter 8

CONCLUSION

TPA expired on July 1, 2007, but the issue of its renewal awaits congressional consideration. This report reviews what FTAs the administration pursued under TPA. The systematic review this report provides forms part of the historical record of what was achieved with this important grant of authority. This report also examines how well the congressional and private sector consultations worked in practice. Although these are considered an essential check to ensure substantively sound and well-supported agreements, our report finds room for improvement.

Under this TPA authority, we found USTR has pursued bilateral and subregional FTAs in order to advance both foreign policy and economic policy goals and as building blocks to larger regional initiatives and global trade expansion. While many in Congress and U.S. industry have supported these FTA negotiations, some have been concerned about the limited economic and commercial benefits gained. However, the U.S. standard of only negotiating comprehensive FTAs has had implications for the universe of suitable trading partners. Certain larger trading partners like the EU and Japan have been unwilling to open up sensitive sectors such as agriculture bilaterally. Negotiations with some larger developing country partners such as Brazil were ultimately abandoned, in part because they were unwilling to accept the comprehensive template proposed by the United States on such topics, as well as intellectual property rights and services. The results in terms of trade coverage illustrate the limitations of pursuing comprehensive FTAs: those in force or concluded under TPA accounted for just 8 percent of total U.S. trade. Yet, after the EU, Japan, and China, the trade partners that remain to be covered by FTAs each account for relatively small shares of U.S. trade.

TPA required that the administration consult with Congress as USTR negotiated trade agreements. We found that USTR provided extensive consultations on FTAs, numbering well over a thousand, over the past 5 years—a significant expenditure of effort, resources, and time for an office of about 200 staff. However, while some current and former congressional committee staff we spoke with were satisfied with the consultations, others still came away feeling that they had not been truly consulted, particularly staff outside of the trade committees. Current and former USTR negotiators we interviewed believed that congressional input was constantly being factored into their discussions, but said lack of early focus by Congress on agreement details often complicated USTR's ability to incorporate congressional input. Clearly, clarification of expectations on both sides is essential to any renewal of TPA.

Certain procedural issues also hampered consultations. For example, most committee staff, particularly outside the trade and agriculture committees, often did not feel that they had the time they needed to review the information USTR shared with them on the status of the negotiations and, in turn, provide meaningful input. Although USTR reports that it has already taken the step of providing committee staff that have security clearances with the negotiating text 5 days in advance, several committee staff told us they frequently have less time. Staff also need to obtain security clearances if they want to be able to access the classified negotiating text; however, some key staff still lack clearances. In addition, some staff with clearances are only able to access text through a cumbersome paper process, while others enjoy electronic access through USTR's secure Web site. Discussing changes from previously proposed text also appears essential to ensuring trust and effective communication. However, both committee staff and former USTR negotiators commented that process changes alone cannot resolve the issues at the heart of the consultation controversy. They said that the political will to engage in meaningful consultations is key and that consultations only work as well as the political relations and good faith of players.

Just over half of the private sector advisory committee chairs we spoke with said they were adequately consulted and told us that having direct access to administration officials is valuable. Nevertheless, our work suggests that tight reporting time frames and delays in finalizing text often compromise committees' ability to provide an advisory opinion within 30 days as to whether agreements promote U.S. economic interests, achieve negotiating goals, and provide for equity and reciprocity, as TPA required. The ITC faces similar challenges in securing text or agreement details that can impede its ability to prepare required reports within statutory time frames. Finally, delays in both committee rechartering and member appointments have led to prolonged lapses in some committees' ability to convene and provide advice. Current reporting by the administration on the trade advisory committee status does not provide sufficient transparency, so Congress may be unaware of some committees' inability to meet and how statutory representation requirements are achieved. As a result, to effectively perform the unique role in U.S. trade policy Congress has given trade advisory committees, certain process issues need to be resolved.

Chapter 9

MATTER FOR CONGRESSIONAL CONSIDERATION

To assist the U.S. Trade Representative and the other agencies in improving the operations and input of the trade advisory committees, Congress should consider extending the reporting deadlines for the trade advisory committees and the ITC by 15 days, giving them 45 days and 195 days, respectively.

Chapter 10

RECOMMENDATIONS FOR EXECUTIVE ACTION

To facilitate better consultations with Congress, we recommend that the U.S. Trade Representative:

- Take steps to reach agreement with the committees of jurisdiction on the amount of time they need to receive information in advance of consultation meetings in order to afford them better opportunity for meaningful input, and
- Work together with Congress on ways to improve access to information prior to consultation meetings, such as through security clearances, so that congressional staff can better assess the status of negotiations and provide advice to USTR.

To provide transparency and accountability to the composition of the trade advisory committees, we recommend that the Secretaries of Agriculture, Commerce, and Labor work with the U.S. Trade Representative to annually report publicly on how they meet the representation requirements of FACA and the Trade Act of 1974, including clarifying which interest members represent in a manner similar to the Department of Commerce and explaining how they determined which representatives they placed on committees.

To assure Congress that it is receiving the private sector advisory opinions that it intended in the Trade Act of 1974, we recommend that the Secretaries of Agriculture and Labor work with the U.S. Trade Representative to take the following two actions:

- Start the advisory committee rechartering and member appointment processes with sufficient time to avoid any lapse in the ability to hold committee meetings, and
- Notify Congress if a committee is unable to meet for more than 3 months due to an expired charter or a delay in the member appointment process.

To promote greater efficiency in trade advisory committee function, we recommend that the Secretary of Labor work with the U.S. Trade Representative to extend the Labor Advisory Committee charter from 2 years to 4 years, to be in alignment with the rest of the trade advisory committee system.

Appendix I

OBJECTIVES, SCOPE, AND METHODOLOGY

To determine how Trade Promotion Authority (TPA) has been used in negotiation of free trade agreements (FTA), we reviewed: (1) What FTAs have been pursued under TPA and why? (2) Overall, what is the economic significance of these agreements to the United States? (3) What is the nature of the consultation process for Congress, and how well has it worked in practice? (4) What is the nature of the consultation process for trade advisory committees and other stakeholders, and how well has it worked in practice?

To answer these questions, generally we reviewed documents and interviewed officials responsible for international trade policy and negotiations at the Office of the U.S. Trade Representative (USTR); the Departments of Agriculture, Commerce, Labor, State, and the Treasury; and the Environmental Protection Agency, as well as officials of the U.S. International Trade Commission (ITC).

To determine what FTAs have been pursued under TPA and why, we reviewed USTR documents and interagency memoranda discussing FTA partner selection and updated our findings from our prior work on FTA partner selection.[1] We also interviewed relevant executive branch agency officials, both current and former, in order to gain the perspectives of those officials involved with the earlier FTAs negotiated under TPA. In addition, we interviewed congressional staff from the House and Senate trade and agriculture committees, as well as other committees of jurisdiction, and over half of the trade advisory committee chairs, in order to learn what input they had into the partner selection process.

To determine the overall economic significance of these FTAs, we analyzed official U.S. trade and investment data, as well as selected studies and analyses from USTR, ITC, and trade experts. U.S. goods trade statistics are from the

Bureau of the Census, and are through 2006. U.S. services trade and investment statistics are from the Bureau of Economic Analysis, and are through 2005, which is the most recent year available. For the purpose of analyzing the overall U.S. trade and investment relationship with TPA and non-TPA trade partners, we determined that these data are sufficiently reliable. Where we combined the two data sets to show the share of total trade (imports plus exports of goods plus services), the modest changes that occur from year to year would only have a minimal effect on the shares reported and no effect on the overall findings. We also grouped detailed U.S. goods trade statistics into two broad categories: agriculture and manufacturing based on the Harmonized Tariff Schedule product chapters. Chapters 1 through 24 are agriculture and the remaining nonagricultural chapters are manufacturing. ITC maintains the official U.S. tariff schedule. A complete list of the product chapters of the Harmonized Tariff schedule can be found at www.usitc.gov. Finally, in order to analyze the growth of U.S. goods trade flows over time we used Bureau of Labor Statistics import and export price deflators at the most disaggregated level available to adjust U.S. trade statistics for inflation from 1992 to 2006. We did not adjust U.S. services statistics since reliable price deflators are not available for the time period we examined.

To determine the nature of the congressional consultation process and how well it has worked in practice, we reviewed fast track provisions from the Trade Act of 1974 up through TPA to trace the evolution of the consultation provisions. We also analyzed USTR's congressional consultation logs in order to determine which committees USTR had provided with consultation meetings, how often, and on which FTAs. We interviewed USTR officials about how the log was compiled and generally found them sufficiently reliable for the purposes of this report. In addition, we interviewed current and former USTR officials who had been involved in providing the FTA consultations, as well as current and former staff of congressional committees that had participated in these consultation meetings, in order to obtain their descriptions of the consultation process and their views on what had worked well and what could be improved. In our congressional interviews, we interviewed both House and Senate committees, including both majority and minority staffs, of all the trade, agriculture, and other committees of jurisdiction that had been involved in these consultations. The committees of jurisdiction comprised the following:

- Senate Finance and House Ways and Means,
- Senate Agriculture, Nutrition, and Forestry and House Agriculture,
- Senate Commerce, Science and Transportation and House Natural Resources (fisheries subcommittees),

- Senate and House Judiciary (intellectual property rights subcommittees),
- Senate Banking, Housing, and Urban Affairs and House Financial Services,
- Senate Commerce, Science and Transportation (telecommunications staff) and House Energy and Commerce (telecommunications subcommittee),
- Senate Homeland Security and Governmental Affairs and House Oversight and Government Reform.

Of the 28 committee staffs (from 7 Senate committees and 7 House committees, each with majority and minority staffs) that we contacted, staff of 18 (64 percent) agreed to be interviewed. The views of the committee staff we interviewed are not necessarily representative to all relevant Senate and House Committees. We interviewed staff of all 4 trade committee staffs, as well as 4 former trade committee staff in order to assure coverage back to the beginning of TPA in 2002, due to staff turnover on some committees. We also interviewed former committee staff of the other committees of jurisdiction when there had been turnover on the staff and the current staff were not sufficiently familiar with the process to comment and referred us to the appropriate former staff.

To determine the nature of the consultation process for the trade advisory committees and how well it worked in practice, we reviewed relevant provisions in the Trade Act of 1974,[2] the Federal Advisory Committee Act (FACA),[3] and TPA[4] governing the establishment and function of the committees as well as their reporting requirements and time frames. We obtained and analyzed committee meeting records and charter and roster information from both designated agency officials and through the FACA database maintained by the General Services Administration. We interviewed a nongeneralizable sampling of 27 trade advisory committee chairs.[5] We interviewed the first tier and all of the relevant second tier chairs. For the third tier, we interviewed a judgmental sample of half of the chairs—half of the agricultural technical advisory committee chairs and half of the industry trade advisory committee chairs—representing a cross section of both agriculture and industry, as well as select committee members referred to us by the chairs for their alternative views.

Altogether, we interviewed 16 of the 27 chairs and 5 additional members. The views of the trade advisory committee chairs with whom we spoke are not necessarily representative of all committee chairs. We also selected four other stakeholders to interview, based on literature and background research, recommendations from trade experts, and participation in public hearings held for each FTA. These stakeholders were trade experts in the nongovernmental organization and academic communities. In addition, we interviewed the executive branch agency officials responsible for overseeing the committees, at USTR and the Departments of Agriculture, Commerce, and Labor. We also interviewed agency officials from the ITC. Finally, we updated findings from our prior work on the trade advisory committees through interviews and document review and analysis.[6]

We conducted our work from January 2007 to August 2007 in accordance with generally accepted government auditing standards.

Appendix II

EXPANSION OF CONGRESSIONAL CONSULTATION REQUIREMENTS AND ROLE OF GATEKEEPER PROVISION

This appendix briefly reviews the evolution of congressional consultation requirements under TPA. In general, consultation requirements have expanded under each renewal of authority. The Trade Act of 1974 was the first grant of fast track authority, which later became known as trade promotion authority.[1] It established the basic consultation framework, including required notifications, consultations with congressional committees, the advisory committee system, and the accreditation of 10 Members of Congress to serve as official advisors to the U.S. delegation of negotiators. The Trade Agreements Act of 1979 extended fast track authority but made no significant changes.[2] The next renewal came through the Trade and Tariff Act of 1984.[3] This act added a new requirement that the President notify Congress of intent to begin trade negotiations at least 60 days in advance.[4] Either the House Ways and Means or the Senate Finance committees could deny fast track consideration by disapproving of the negotiation within 60 days of the notification. This provision became known as the "gatekeeper" provision. In at least one instance, Congress reportedly used the provision as a tool to successfully influence the administration.[5]

The Omnibus Trade and Competitiveness Act of 1988 continued the previous consultation requirements and added that the Congress could withhold a trade agreement from fast track consideration by passing resolutions of disapproval if it determined that the President had failed to adequately consult with Congress.[6] In addition, the 1988 act extended fast track procedures only for 3 years but allowed an extension of fast track procedures for an additional 2 years if the

President requested the extension, and Congress did not pass a resolution disapproving of the extension. The Trade Act of 2002 included all of the consultation requirements of previous acts with the exception of the gatekeeper provision.[7] Instead of giving the two main trade committees the power to essentially veto potential trading partners before negotiations begin, the 2002 act replaced the 60-day notification of intent to begin negotiations with a 90-day notification. The Trade Act of 2002 also established the Congressional Oversight Group (COG) as an additional consultation mechanism.[8]

Appendix III

DETAILED INFORMATION ON U.S. GOODS AND SERVICES TRADE, INVESTMENT, AND TARIFFS OF U.S. TRADE PARTNERS

This appendix provides detailed information on U.S. goods trade (table 5) and services trade (table 6) with U.S. trade partners grouped by whether the United States pursued an FTA with them under TPA, already had an existing FTA with them, or did not pursue an FTA with them. It also provides information on U.S. foreign direct investment in these countries (table 7) and the countries' average applied tariff rates (table 8).

Table 5. U.S. Goods Exports and Imports with Trade Partners

U.S. dollars in millions								
	Exports				Imports			
	Value	Share	Growth		Value	Share	Growth	
Trade partner	2006	2006	1997-2006	2002-2006	2006	2006	1997-2006	2002-2006
			(CAGR)	(CAGR)			(CAGR)	(CAGR)
All countries	929,486	100%	4%	8%	1,845,053	100%	7%	7%
All FTAs pursued under TPA	184,066	20	4	10	269,470	15	6	6
FTAs concluded and in force	60,999	7	5	8	51,470	3	5	6
Australia	16,836	2	4	6	8,244	0	3	-1
Bahrain	471	0	0	1	632	0	19	9
Singapore	21,911	2	5	8	17,750	1	5	9
Chile	6,221	1	4	26	9,551	1	13	17
Morocco	869	0	7	8	546	0	3	-1
CAFTA-DR	14,691	2	6	6	14,746	1	4	2
Dominican Republic	5,033	1	4	3	4,540	0	0	0
El Salvador	2,083	0	4	5	1,843	0	4	-3
Guatemala	3,299	0	7	10	3,103	0	4	-1
Honduras	3,571	0	7	7	3,735	0	6	3
Nicaragua	705	0	11	12	1,526	0	14	20
FTAs concluded but not yet in force	46,918	5	3	9	64,784	4	7	5
Colombia	6,236	1	2	13	9,240	1	0	-3
Costa Rica	3,877	0	9	8	3,813	0	6	4
Oman	832	0	11	21	782	0	8	7
Panama	2,524	0	3	10	338	0	-1	-4
Peru	2,655	0	4	13	5,897	0	8	14
South Korea	30,794	3	3	8	44,714	2	10	6
FTAs pursued but not yet concluded	76,149	8	3	13	153,216	8	6	7

Table 5. (Continued).

U.S. dollars in millions								
	Exports				Imports			
	Value	Share	Growth		Value	Share	Growth	
Trade partner	2006	2006	1997-2006 (CAGR)	2002-2006 (CAGR)	2006	2006	1997-2006 (CAGR)	2002-2006 (CAGR)
FTAA	41,873	5	1	12	84,687	5	3	4
Brazil	16,977	2	1	8	26,169	1	9	7
Argentina	4,271	0	-3	25	3,925	0	1	-10
Venezuela	8,476	1	2	17	36,283	2	-1	1
Ecuador	2,548	0	4	11	7,011	0	7	17
Other	9,600	1	4	10	11,298	1	10	9
Thailand	7,526	1	1	13	22,345	1	9	10
Malaysia	11,164	1	3	7	36,441	2	12	15
United Arab Emirates	11,197	1	17	31	1,314	0	3	2
SACU	4,389	0	4	12	8,429	0	8	8
Botswana	27	0	-6	-5	252	0	28	68
Lesotho	4	0	6	20	408	0	19	6
Namibia	113	0	20	16	116	0	4	4
South Africa	4,234	0	3	12	7,497	0	8	7
Swaziland	11	0	11	20	156	0	14	8
FTAs prior to TPA	321,506	35	5	6	520,668	28	5	4
Israel	8,094	1	6	11	19,157	1	11	10
Jordan	623	0	5	10	1,421	0	54	35
NAFTA	312,789	34	5	6	500,090	27	5	4
Canada	198,226	21	4	7	303,034	16	4	2
Mexico	114,562	12	6	5	197,056	11	8	6
Non-FTA countries	423,914	46	4	9	1,054,916	57	8	9
EU	197,281	21	4	8	330,898	18	7	5
Japan	55,596	6	-1	1	148,071	8	3	5
China	51,624	6	17	23	287,052	16	19	23

Table 5. (Continued).

U.S. dollars in millions								
	Exports				Imports			
	Value	Share	Growth		Value	Share	Growth	
Trade partner	2006	2006	1997-2006	2002-2006	2006	2006	1997-2006	2002-2006
			(CAGR)	(CAGR)			(CAGR)	(CAGR)
India	9,025	1	10	22	21,674	1	12	12
All others	110,389	12%	2%	9%	267,221	14%	5%	7%

Legend

CAFTA-DR = Central America-Dominican Republic Free Trade Agreement FTAA = Free Trade Area of the Americas NAFTA = North American Free Trade Agreement SACU = Southern African Customs Union

Source: GAO analysis of official U.S. trade statistics from the U.S. Census Bureau.

Notes: CAGR stands for Compound Annual Growth Rate. “0%” represents values that are less than 0.5 percent and therefore round to zero.

Table 6. U.S. Services Exports and Imports with Trade Partners

U.S. dollars in millions	Exports				Imports			
	Value	Share	Growth		Value	Share	Growth	
Trade partner	2005	2005	1996-2005	2002-2005	2005	2005	2005	2005
			(CAGR)	(CAGR)			(CAGR)	(CAGR)
All countries	360,489	100%	6%	9%	280,563	100%	8%	10%
All FTAs pursued under TPA	63,051	17	4	5	41,689	15	6	11
FTAs concluded and in force	14,509	4	5	6	9,104	3	7	16
Australia	7,409	2	6	12	4,660	2	7	15
Bahrain	n.a.	n.a.	n.a.	n.a.	n.a.	n.a.	n.a.	n.a.
Singapore	5,753	2	5	1	3,726	1	8	22
Chile	1,347	0	1	4	718	0	4	0
Morocco	n.a.	n.a.	n.a.	n.a.	n.a.	n.a.	n.a.	n.a.
CAFTA-DR	n.a.	n.a.	n.a.	n.a.	n.a.	n.a.	n.a.	n.a.
Dominican Republic	n.a.	n.a.	n.a.	n.a.	n.a.	n.a.	n.a.	n.a.
El Salvador	n.a.	n.a.	n.a.	n.a.	n.a.	n.a.	n.a.	n.a.
Guatemala	n.a.	n.a.	n.a.	n.a.	n.a.	n.a.	n.a.	n.a.
Honduras	n.a.	n.a.	n.a.	n.a.	n.a.	n.a.	n.a.	n.a.
Nicaragua	n.a.	n.a.	n.a.	n.a.	n.a.	n.a.	n.a.	n.a.
FTAs concluded but not yet in								
force	10,298	3	4	9	6,305	2	5	13
Colombia	n.a.	n.a.	n.a.	n.a.	n.a.	n.a.	n.a.	n.a.
Costa Rica	n.a.	n.a.	n.a.	n.a.	n.a.	n.a.	n.a.	n.a.
Oman	n.a.	n.a.	n.a.	n.a.	n.a.	n.a.	n.a.	n.a.
Panama	n.a.	n.a.	n.a.	n.a.	n.a.	n.a.	n.a.	n.a.
Peru	n.a.	n.a.	n.a.	n.a.	n.a.	n.a.	n.a.	n.a.
South Korea	10,298	3	4	9	6,305	2	5	13
FTAs pursued but not yet								
concluded	38,245	11	4	3	26,280	9	5	9
FTAA	33,946	9	4	3	23,562	8	5	9
Brazil	5,852	2	1	5	2,075	1	4	6

Table 6. Continued.

U.S. dollars in millions	Exports				Imports			
	Value	Share	Growth		Value	Share	Growth	
Trade partner	2005	2005	1996-2005	2002-2005	2005	2005	2005	2005
			(CAGR)	(CAGR)			(CAGR)	(CAGR)
Argentina	1,813	1	-5	4	792	0	0	11
Venezuela	2,637	1	1	-2	580	0	-3	8
Ecuador	n.a.	n.a.	n.a.	n.a.	n.a.	n.a.	n.a.	n.a.
Other	23,644	7	6	3	20,115	7	6	9
Thailand	1,507	0	2	9	1,090	0	3	11
Malaysia	1,373	0	1	6	708	0	5	13
United Arab Emirates	n.a.	n.a.	n.a.	n.a.	n.a.	n.a.	n.a.	n.a.
SACU	1,418	0	6	6	920	0	6	7
Botswana	n.a.	n.a.	n.a.	n.a.	n.a.	n.a.	n.a.	n.a.
Lesotho	n.a.	n.a.	n.a.	n.a.	n.a.	n.a.	n.a.	n.a.
Namibia	n.a.	n.a.	n.a.	n.a.	n.a.	n.a.	n.a.	n.a.
South Africa	1,418	0	6	6	920	0	6	7
Swaziland	n.a.	n.a.	n.a.	n.a.	n.a.	n.a.	n.a.	n.a.
FTAs prior to TPA	55,821	15	7	9	39,097	14	6	8
Israel	2,711	1	4	6	2,401	1	6	16
Jordan	n.a.	n.a.	n.a.	n.a.	n.a.	n.a.	n.a.	n.a.
NAFTA	53,110	15	7	9	36,696	13	6	7
Canada	32,506	9	6	9	22,022	8	7	7
Mexico	20,604	6	9	9	14,674	5	6	8
Non-FTA countries	241,617	67	6	10	199,776	71	9	11
EU	127,840	35	7	10	105,902	38	9	10
Japan	41,815	12	3	11	22,287	8	6	9
China	9,078	3	12	15	6,505	2	14	16
India	5,193	1	15	17	5,018	2	18	40
All others	57,691	16%	5%	8%	60,064	21%	9%	10%

Table 6. Continued

Legend
CAFTA-DR = Central America-Dominican Republic Free Trade Agreement
FTAA = Free Trade Area of the Americas
NAFTA = North American Free Trade Agreement
SACU = Southern African Customs Union

Source: GAO analysis of official private services trade statistics from the Bureau of Economic Analysis.

Notes: "n.a." indicates that data was not reported by the Bureau of Economic Analysis (BEA) for these countries. The values for "FTAA (other)" are based on BEA's categories "Other South and Central America" and "Other Western Hemisphere," excluding countries already listed in this table and Bermuda. Growth rates are based on nominal values. U.S. trade in services statistics are through 2005, which is the most recent year available.

Table 7. U.S. Direct Investment Abroad (Foreign Direct Investment) by Trade Partner

U.S. dollars in millions	Value	Share	Growth	
Trade partner	2005	2005	1996-2005	2002-2005
			(CAGR)	(CAGR)
All countries	2,069,983	100%	11%	9%
All FTAs pursued under TPA	321,871	16	9	13
FTAs concluded and in force	174,438	8	14	20
Australia	113,385	5	16	43
Bahrain	194	0	204	40
Singapore	48,051	2	14	-2
Chile	9,811	0	2	3
Morocco	285	0	12	1
CAFTA-DR	2,712	0	15	4
Dominican Republic	758	0	7	-8
El Salvador	928	0	20	12
Guatemala	379	0	n.a.	8

Table 7. Continued.

U.S. dollars in millions	Value	Share	Growth	
Trade partner	2005	2005	1996-2005	2002-2005
			(CAGR)	(CAGR)
Honduras	402	0	13	30
Nicaragua	245	0	13	-1
FTAs concluded but not yet in force	33,106	2	1	9
Colombia	3,393	0	0	9
Costa Rica	1,277	0	0	-11
Oman	615	0	26	47
Panama	5,162	0	-12	-4
Peru	3,900	0	6	6
South Korea	18,759	1	12	17
FTAs pursued but not yet concluded	114,327	6	6	5
FTAA	89,432	4	5	4
Brazil	32,420	2	1	6
Argentina	13,163	1	6	5
Venezuela	9,610	0	9	3
Ecuador	760	0	-2	-2
Other	33,479	2	9	3
Thailand	8,556	0	6	3
Malaysia	9,993	0	7	12
United Arab Emirates	2,663	0	18	35
SACU	3,683	0	10	3
Botswana	5	0	-16	n.a.
Lesotho	3	0	13	0
Namibia	n.a.	n.a.	n.a.	n.a.
South Africa	3,594	0	10	3
Swaziland	81	0	n.a	n.a.
FTAs prior to TPA	314,170	15	12	11
Israel	7,920	0	16	11

Table 7. Continued.

U.S. dollars in millions	Value	Share	Growth	
Trade partner	2005	2005	1996-2005 (CAGR)	2002-2005 (CAGR)
Jordan	-4	0	n.a.	n.a.
NAFTA	306,254	15	12	11
Canada	234,831	11	11	12
Mexico	71,423	3	16	8
Non-FTA countries	1,433,942	69	12	7
EU	949,809	46	12	7
Japan	75,491	4	9	4
China	16,877	1	18	17
India	8,456	0	23	26
All others	383,309	19%	12%	7%

Legend

CAFTA-DR = Central America-Dominican Republic Free Trade Agreement FTAA = Free Trade Area of the Americas NAFTA = North American Free Trade Agreement SACU = Southern African Customs Union

Source: GAO analysis of official U.S. direct investment abroad statistics from the Bureau of Economic Analysis.

Notes: "n.a." indicates that data was not reported by the Bureau of Economic Analysis (BEA) for these countries.

The values for "FTAA (other)" are based on BEA's categories "South America," "Central America," and "Other Western Hemisphere," excluding countries already listed in this table or not a part of the FTAA negotiations. Values are direct investment position (stock) on an historical cost basis.

Growth rates are based on nominal values.

U.S. direct investment abroad statistics are through 2005, which is the most recent year available.

Table 8. Most Favored Nation Applied Tariff Rates by Trade Partner

Trade partner	All products	Agriculture	Nonagriculture
All FTAs pursued under TPA			
FTAs concluded and in force			
Australia	3.5%	1.2%	3.9%
Bahrain	5.1	7.2	4.8
Singapore	0.0	0.2	0.0
Chile	6.0	6.0	6.0
Morocco	24.5	46.2	21.2
CAFTA-DR			
Dominican Republic	8.5	13.1	7.8
El Salvador	5.9	11.5	5.0
Guatemala	5.6	9.7	5.0
Honduras	5.6	9.9	4.9
Nicaragua	5.6	10.6	4.9
FTAs concluded but not yet in force			
Colombia	12.5	16.6	11.8
Costa Rica	5.9	12.3	4.9
Oman	5.3	8.7	4.8
Panama	7.3	13.6	6.4
Peru	10.2	13.6	9.7
South Korea	12.1	47.8	6.6
FTAs pursued but not yet concluded			
FTAA			
Brazil	12.3	10.2	12.6
Argentina	12.2	10.1	12.6
Venezuela	n.a.	n.a.	n.a.
Ecuador	n.a.	n.a.	n.a.
Other	n.a.	n.a.	n.a.
Thailand	10.0	22.1	8.2
Malaysia	8.5	12.3	7.9

Table 8. (Continued).

Trade partner	All products	Agriculture	Nonagriculture
United Arab Emirates	5.0	6.5	4.8
SACU			
Botswana	8.0	9.3	7.8
Lesotho	7.9	9.0	7.8
Namibia	8.0	9.2	7.8
South Africa	8.0	9.0	7.9
Swaziland	8.0	9.3	7.8
FTAs prior to TPA			
Israel	6.5	17.1	4.9
Jordan	11.5	18.1	10.4
NAFTA			
Canada	5.5	17.3	3.7
Mexico	14.0	18.2	13.3
Non-FTA countries			
EU	5.4	15.1	3.9
Japan	5.6	24.3	2.8
China	9.9	15.7	9.0
India	19.2	37.6	16.4
Addendum			
United States	3.5%	5.3%	3.3%

Legend

CAFTA-DR = Central America-Dominican Republic Free Trade Agreement FTAA = Free Trade Area of the Americas NAFTA = North American Free Trade Agreement SACU = Southern African Customs Union Source: World Trade Organization, World Tariff Profiles 2006.

Note: Applied rates listed in this table are based on the simple average of ad valorem most favored nation rates. It does not include non ad valorem duties unless ad valorem equivalent rates were available.

Appendix IV

COMPARISON OF U.S. TRADE AND INVESTMENT WITH FTA AND NON-FTA PARTNERS

The U.S. trade and investment relationship with countries that the United States has chosen to pursue FTAs under TPA differs from that with non-FTA countries in several ways.[1] The United States tends to (1) maintain more balanced trade with TPA countries, (2) export relatively more manufactured goods (compared with services and agriculture), and (3) have relatively faster investment growth with TPA countries, particularly in countries with FTAs in force.

U.S. MAINTAINS MORE BALANCED TRADE WITH TPA COUNTRIES

The overall U.S. trade deficit has been large and growing for many years. Much of the gap between exports and imports has been driven by increased imports from Asian countries, including China and Japan.[2] In contrast, the United States has relatively more balanced trade with the group of countries pursued under TPA. Figure 9 shows the goods trade balances for TPA countries, existing FTA partners (e.g., Canada and Mexico), and non-FTA countries (e.g., EU, Japan, China, India). The trade balance with TPA countries is in deficit overall, but the deficit is relatively smaller and has deteriorated less rapidly than the much larger deficit with non-FTA countries.[3]

Moreover, the trends in the U.S. trade deficit vary across the groups of countries pursued under TPA. For TPA countries with which the United States has put in force the FTA agreements (e.g., Australia, Chile, CAFTA-DR), the goods trade balance is in surplus. Figure 10 shows TPA countries by the status of the FTA negotiations: in force, concluded but not yet in force, and pursued but not yet concluded. For FTA agreements that have been put in force, the United States maintains a small but growing trade surplus. For agreements that have been concluded but not yet in force, the United States maintains a trade deficit that has declined in recent years. Finally, for countries in which the United States pursued an FTA agreement, but has not yet completed negotiations, the trade deficit has been negative and growing.

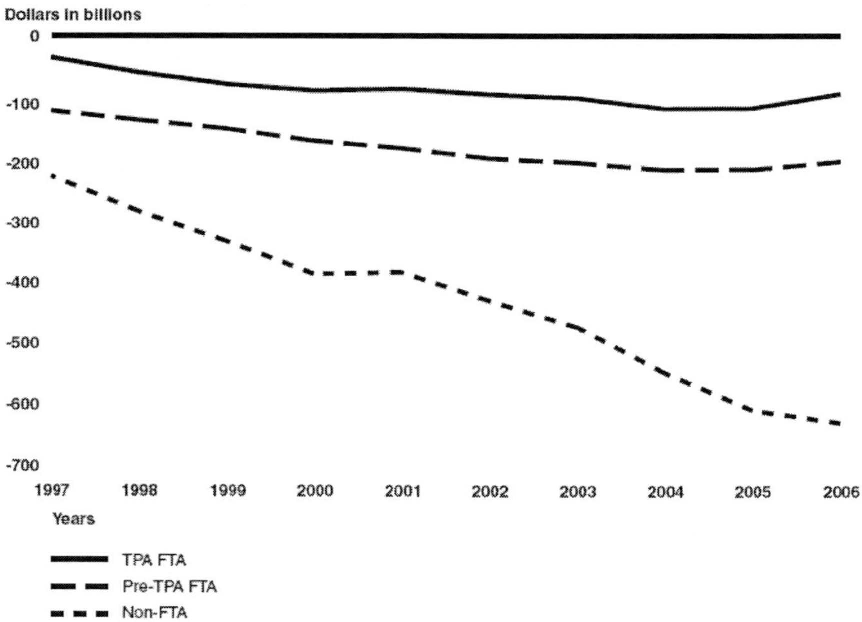

Source: GAO analysis of official U.S. trade statistics from the U.S. Census Bureau.

Figure 9. U.S. Goods Trade Balance (Exports–Imports) with TPA Countries, Existing FTAs, and Non-FTA Countries, 1997-2006.

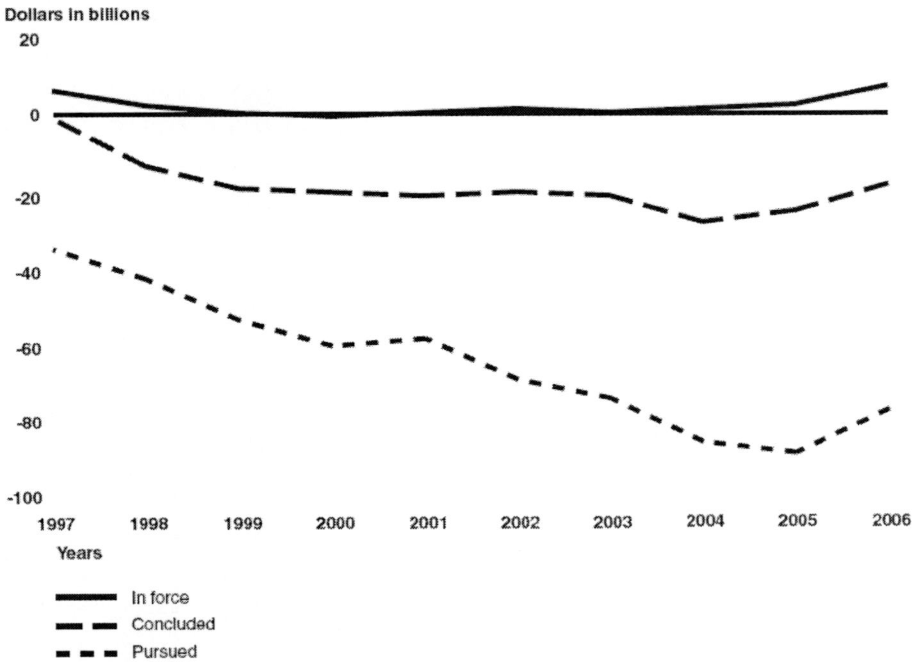

Source: GAO analysis of official U.S. trade statistics from the U.S. Census Bureau.

Figure 10. U.S. Goods Trade Balance (Exports–Imports) with TPA Countries, by Status of FTA Negotiations, 1997-2006.

U.S. Exports More Manufacturing and Imports More Agricultural Products with TPA Countries

Relative to services and agriculture, manufacturing products comprise a higher share of total U.S. exports to TPA countries (70 percent) compared with non-FTA countries (59 percent), as shown in figure 11. This is mirrored by a relatively smaller share of services exports to TPA countries (26 percent) compared with non-FTA countries (36 percent). In addition, while U.S. manufacturing exports to both TPA and non-FTA countries are growing at similar rates (between 10-11 percent annually, from 2002–2006 based on a compound annual growth rate), U.S. services exports to TPA countries are growing more slowly than U.S. services exports to non-FTA countries (5 percent for TPA countries, versus 10 percent for non-FTA countries). Table 6 in appendix III shows growth rates for services trade.

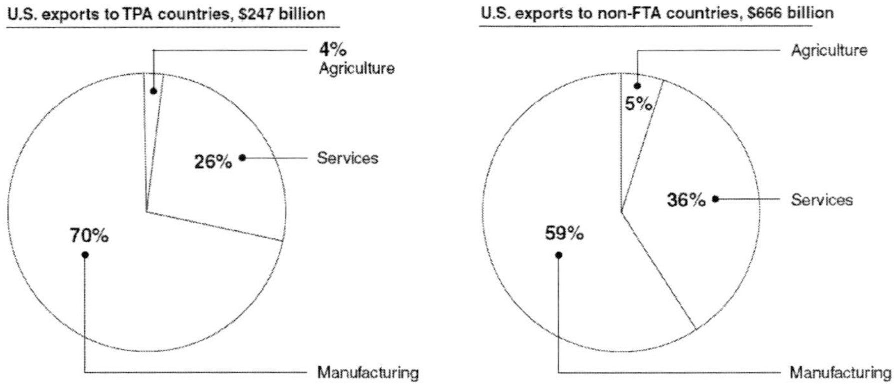

Source: GAO analysis of official U.S. trade statistics from the U.S. Census Bureau.

Notes: Figures based on U.S. trade with all countries pursued under TPA (TPA countries) and U.S. trade with countries not pursued under TPA and with which the U.S. does not currently have an FTA (non-FTA countries).

Manufacturing includes all nonagricultural goods trade. U.S. trade in goods statistics are for 2006. U.S. trade in services statistics are for 2005, which is the most recent year available. See appendix I for more information on our methodology and product composition.

Figure 11. Comparison of U.S. Exports to TPA Countries Versus Non-FTA Countries.

In terms of U.S. imports, manufacturing products comprise a much larger share of both TPA and non-FTA imports—80 and 82 percent, respectively, than manufacturing comprises in U.S. exports to these groups. Figure 12 shows the composition of U.S. imports from both groups. While U.S. services imports are relatively similar for TPA and non-FTA countries, agricultural imports from TPA countries (7 percent) are much larger as a share of total imports from TPA countries, compared to non-FTA countries (2 percent). In addition, agricultural imports from TPA countries have also been growing faster (9 percent annually) compared to imports of agricultural products from non-FTA countries (6 percent annually) from 2002 to 2006, based on a compound annual growth rate.

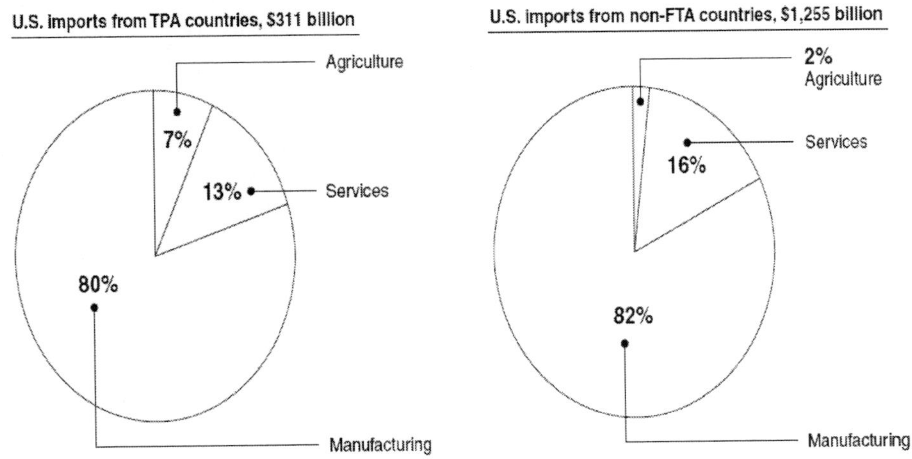

Source: GAO analysis of official U.S. trade statistics from the U.S. Census Bureau.

Notes: Figures based on U.S. trade with all countries pursued under TPA (TPA countries) and U.S. trade with countries not pursued under TPA and with which the United States does not currently have an FTA (non-FTA countries)

Manufacturing includes all nonagricultural goods trade. U.S. trade in goods statistics are for 2006. U.S. trade in services statistics are for 2005, which is the most recent year available. See appendix I for more information on our methodology and product composition.

Figure 12. Comparison of U.S. Imports from TPA Countries Versus Non-FTA Countries by Product Group.

U.S. Investment in TPA Countries Growing Relatively Rapidly Since Completion of FTAs

U.S. direct investment abroad (or foreign direct investment, FDI) in TPA countries has grown more rapidly than investment in non-FTA countries, particularly in recent years since the conclusion of FTA agreements. Table 9 shows that U.S. FDI in TPA countries registered a compound annual growth rate of 9 percent between 1996 and 2005, and a 13 percent compound annual growth rate since 2002. For TPA countries in which an FTA with the United States is already in force, the compound annual growth rate was 20 percent from 2002 to 2005. In comparison, U.S. direct investment in non-FTA countries grew at a compound annual growth rate of 7 percent over the same period.

Table 9. U.S. Direct Investment Abroad (Foreign Direct Investment) by Trade Partner Group

U.S. dollars in millions				
	Value	Share	Growth	
Trade partner	2005	2005	1996-2005	2002-2005
			(CAGR)	(CAGR)
All countries	2,069,983	100%	11%	9%
All FTAs under TPA	321,871	16	9	13
FTAs concluded and in force	174,438	8	14	20
FTAs concluded but not yet in force	33,106	2	1	9
FTAs prior to TPA	314,170	15	12	11
Non-FTA countries	1,433,942	69%	12%	7%

Source: GAO analysis of official U.S. direct investment abroad statistics from the Bureau of Economic Analysis.

Note: Growth rates are based on nominal values.

REFERENCES

[1] Pub. L. No. 107-210, Div. B, 116 Stat. 933, 993–1022 (codified at 19 U.S.C. §§ 3801-13).

[2] Launched in November 2001 in Doha, Qatar, these negotiations involve 150 nations and encompass a far-reaching agenda for liberalizing trade and bolstering development in poorer countries. Among other things, they involve efforts to reach agreement to reduce barriers such as tariffs (border taxes) and trade-distorting subsidies on agriculture, manufactures, and services trade. For further background see www.wto.org and GAO, *World Trade Organization: Congress Faces Key Decisions as Efforts to Reach Doha Agreement Intensify*, GAO-07-379 (Washington, D.C.: Mar. 5, 2007).

[3] See GAO, *International Trade: Intensifying Free Trade Negotiating Agenda Calls for Better Allocation of Staff and Resources*, GAO-04-233 (Washington, D.C.: Jan. 12, 2004).

[4] *See* Trade Act of 1974, Pub. L. No. 93-618, 88 Stat. 1978 (1975); Trade Agreement Act of 1979, Pub. L. No. 96-39, 93 Stat. 144; Trade and Tariff Act of 1984, Pub. L. No. 98-573, 98 Stat. 2948; Omnibus Trade and Competitiveness Act of 1988, Pub. L. No. 100-418, 102 Stat. 1107; Trade Act of 2002, Pub. L. No. 107-210, 116 Stat. 933.

[5] Pub. L. No. 93-618.

[6] Pub. L. No. 92-463, 86 Stat. 770 (1972).

[7] Pub. L. No. 107-210.

[8] GAO, *International Trade: Advisory Committee System Should Be Updated to Better Serve U.S. Policy Needs*, GAO-02-876 (Washington, D.C.; Sept. 24, 2002).

[9] *See*, United States-Chile Free Trade Agreement Implementation Act, Pub. L. No. 108-77, 117 Stat. 909 (2003); United States-Singapore Free Trade

Agreement Implementation Act, Pub. L. No. 108-78, 117 Stat. 948 (2003); United States-Australia Free Trade Agreement Implementation Act, Pub. L. No. 108-286, 118 Stat. 919 (2004); United States-Morocco Free Trade Agreement Implementation Act, Pub. L. No. 108-302, 118 Stat. 1103 (2004); Dominican Republic-Central America-United States Free Trade Agreement Implementation Act, Pub. L. No. 109-53, 119 Stat. 462 (2005); United States-Bahrain Free Trade Agreement Implementation Act, Pub. L. No. 109-169, 119 Stat. 3581 (2006).

[10] Goods trade data are from 2006, while services trade data and investment data are from 2005, which is the most recent year available.

[11] 19 U.S.C. § 3804 (e).

[12] A prerequisite to FTAs entering into force is that the President must notify Congress 90 days before signing the agreement. Advisory committee reports are required to be submitted to Congress not later than 30 days after the Presidential notification of the intention to sign the agreement. *See* 19 U.S.C. §§ 3805(a), 3804(a).

[13] 19 U.S.C. § 2155.

[14] The implementing bill makes the changes in current U.S. law needed to fulfill the terms of the FTA.

[15] Reciprocal Trade Agreements Act of 1934, Pub. L. No. 73-316, 48 Stat. 943.

[16] *See* Trade Act of 1974, Pub. L. No. 93-618; Trade Agreement Act of 1979, Pub. L. No. 96-39; Trade and Tariff Act of 1984, Pub. L. No. 98-573; Omnibus Trade and Competitiveness Act of 1988, Pub. L. No. 100-418; Trade Act of 2002, Pub. L. No. 107-210.

[17] 19 U.S.C. §§ 3801-13.

[18] 19 U.S.C. § 3803 (c)(3).

[19] 19 U.S.C. § 2155 (i).

[20] 19 U.S.C. § 3804 (e).

[21] 19 U.S.C. § 2153.

[22] The Trade Policy Staff Committee is administered and chaired by USTR, and is the subcabinet-level mechanism for developing and coordinating U.S. government positions on international trade and trade-related investment issues.

[23] GAO, *International Trade: Advisory Committee System Should Be Updated to Better Serve U.S. Policy Needs*, GAO-02-876 (Washington, D.C.; Sept. 24, 2002).

[24] Prior to TPA, the United States had already concluded and put into force four FTAs with four countries. Two of those countries, Canada and Mexico,

were also part of the Free Trade Area of the Americas agreement pursued under TPA.

[25] Costa Rica is the only partner country of the Central America-Dominican Republic Free Trade Agreement (CAFTA-DR) that has not yet approved implementing legislation. As CAFTA-DR is already in force for the remaining countries (El Salvador, Honduras, Nicaragua, Guatemala, the Dominican Republic, and the United States), it was not counted as an additional FTA here.

[26] Once a trade agreement on tariff and nontariff barriers, including an FTA, has been concluded and signed by the President under TPA, before the agreement can enter into force, Congress must enact the implementing bill into law. Additionally, the agreement enters into force only once each party has completed the necessary domestic legal procedures (for the United States, this means enactment of the implementing bill into law), and the parties have exchanged written notices that such procedures have been completed.

[27] Agency officials told us that negotiations for these 5 FTAs have not yet been concluded for a variety of reasons. For example, negotiations with SACU were suspended due to a mutual recognition of a lack of readiness, and the United States will be ready to resume negotiations with Thailand once it returns to a democratically elected government.

[28] GAO reported in 2004 that possible FTA partners are proposed through an interagency process, which USTR coordinates. (GAO-04-233). Senior congressional staff, Members of Congress, and trade advisory committee members have also at times provided USTR with informal, unsolicited feedback on FTA partner selection.

[29] 19 U.S.C. §§ 2461-67.

[30] 19 U.S.C. §§ 2701-07.

[31] Trade and Development Act of 2000, Pub. L. No. 106-200, Title I, 114 Stat. 251, 252-275.

[32] 119 U.S.C. §§ 3201-06.

[33] Pub. L. No. 109-53.

[34] Pub. L. No. 106-200, Title II, § 202, 34 Stat. 251, 276 (codified at 19 U.S.C. § 2701 note).

[35] For a more detailed discussion of these differences, see GAO, *World Trade Organization: Congress Faces Key Decisions as Efforts to Reach Doha Agreement Intensify*, GAO-07-379 (Washington, D.C.: Mar. 5, 2007).

[36] With a negative list approach to services, all services sectors and measures would be covered by the agreement unless they are specifically excluded.

With a positive list approach, only services specifically listed would be included in the agreement.

[37] 19 U.S.C. § 2902 (b)(2).

[38] Costa Rica is the only CAFTA partner country that has not yet approved implementing legislation.

[39] See, for example, DeRosa, Dean A and John P. Gilbert, "Technical Appendix: Quantitative Estimates of the Economic Impacts of U.S. Bilateral Free Trade Agreements," in Jeffrey J. Schott, ed., *Free Trade Agreements: US Strategies and Priorities* (Washington, D.C.: Institute for International Economics, April 2004), 383-417.

[40] See U.S. International Trade Commission, U.S.-Korea Free Trade Agreement: Potential Economy-wide and Selected Sectoral Effects (Washington, D.C.: USITC Publication 3949, September 2007) as well as reports of other investigations conducted under Section 2104 of TPA.

[41] For example, see 19 U.S.C. § 2465.

[42] These are simple average tariff rates calculated by the WTO for all tariff lines in which ad valorem (i.e., percentage of price) tariff rates were available. They generally do not include non-ad valorem rates (e.g., specific rates of duty, such as 5 cents per bushel).

[43] Although the term "most favored nation" was replaced domestically with the term "normal trade relations" in 1998, the former is still used in international agreements.

[44] This is cited in WTO's *World Tariff Profiles 2006*. USDA and ITC estimate South Korea's average ad valorem tariff for agricultural goods at 52 percent.

[45] The United States has pursued several FTAs with countries that are small in terms of the size of U.S. trade, including Bahrain and Morocco.

[46] In this report, we compare the trade and investment relationship of the United States with countries pursued under TPA (TPA countries) to countries with which the United States neither has an FTA nor has pursued one under TPA (non-FTA countries). A third group includes those countries with which the United States already had an FTA in effect prior to TPA (FTAs prior to TPA; e.g., NAFTA).

[47] 19 U.S.C. § 3804.

[48] 19 U.S.C. §§ 3804, 3807.

[49] 19 U.S.C. § 3804.

[50] 19 U.S.C. §§ 3804(d)-(f), 3805.

[51] The President "enters into" an international trade agreement when he or she signs it. However, FTAs do not "enter into force" until Congress approves

the implementing bill and all other signatories have taken the measures necessary to come into compliance with the provisions of the agreement that are to take effect on the date on which the agreement enters into force, and the signatories set a date for entry into force.
[52] 19 U.S.C. § 3805(a).
[53] 19 U.S.C. § 3805(b).
[54] 19 U.S.C. § 3803.
[55] 19 U.S.C. § 3805(c).
[56] USTR also held an additional 1,217 consultation meetings related to issues other than FTAs, such as WTO negotiations and trade with China, according to its consultation log.
[57] This is for the entire period of analysis, August 6, 2002 (date of TPA passage)–April 20, 2007. The majority and minority parties switched in January 2007. In addition, the majority party in the Senate switched in January 2003. For the period from August 2002 through December 2002, when the Senate was under Democratic control, and the House was under Republican control, there were 10 majority-only meetings with staff of committees of jurisdiction and 10 minority-only meetings. For the period that accounts for the bulk of the period of analysis, from January 2003 through December 2006, there were 134 majority-only meetings with staff of committees of jurisdiction and 60 minority-only meetings. From January 2007 through April 20, 2007, there were 4 majority-only meetings and 7 minority-only meetings.
[58] 19 U.S.C. § 3807.
[59] We interviewed current and former committee staff of the key committees of jurisdiction. We interviewed former committee staff when there had been turnover on the staff and the current staff were not sufficiently familiar with the process to comment and referred us to the appropriate former staff. For the trade committees, particularly where there had been significant turnover among senior committee staff, we tried to ensure that we spoke with former staff that had been present on the committee back to 2002, when TPA was launched and the initial understandings reached.
[60] Of 28 committee staffs (from seven committees of jurisdiction in each House, each with a majority and minority staff) that we contacted, we were able to secure interviews with individuals from 18. For more information about our methodology, see appendix I.
[61] In characterizing the views of committee staff in our report, we do not hereafter indicate whether the views given were from current or former staff, in order to protect the confidentiality of their views.

[62] The USTR lead negotiators are generally Assistant U.S. Trade Representatives, who are office directors within USTR.

[63] Each congressional committee typically has separate majority and minority professional committee staff, hired by the Chair and Ranking Minority Member, respectively. The other Members of Congress who are committee members generally have legislative assistants from their own personal staff assigned to cover their committee work.

[64] Almost all of the trade committee staff that we interviewed that participated in the consultations had clearances or a lapsed clearance they said they intended to have updated soon.

[65] We spoke with 18 of 28 committee staffs, which is a response rate of 64 percent. The staff that we were able to interview had a larger proportion of majority (now Democratic) staff than minority (now Republican) staff. Given the small number of staff involved and the potential for response bias, we are not characterizing our findings in terms of a specific percentage of respondents.

[66] While this had been a complaint of the trade committees during the early years of TPA, several years ago USTR instituted a 5-day policy whereby text and information were provided to the trade committees at least 5 business days in advance of the consultation meeting. In addition, USTR reported that its policy did not apply just to the trade committees, but that it provided text to staff with security clearances of all committees 5 days in advance. However, several committee staff across a range of committees told us that they frequently have less time. As a result, it is not clear whether this policy has been applied consistently.

[67] Almost all of the committee staff we interviewed from the other committees of jurisdiction either did not feel FTA partner selection was an issue of concern or had no views on the subject.

[68] The gatekeeper provision was a requirement that the President notify Congress of intent to begin trade negotiations at least 60 days in advance. Either the House Ways and Means or the Senate Finance committees could deny fast track consideration by disapproving of the negotiation within 60 days of the notification. See appendix II for additional information about the history of fast track and the role of the gatekeeper provision.

[69] 19 U.S.C. § 2112(4).

[70] Mock markup was instituted because any bill submitted under TPA must be voted on an up-or-down basis without amendment. Before USTR sends up an FTA package for congressional consideration, it sends a draft that includes the signed agreement and a draft of the proposed implementing

bill, as well as other supporting documents. Because the fast track process provides that there will be no amendments to the implementing legislation, the trade committees hold "mock" markups of the draft legislation before it is formally submitted to Congress, so that they can indicate the changes that need to be made before it will be acceptable to the committee. However, the mock markups are nonbinding, allowing USTR to decide against changing the legislative language before sending to Congress for an up or down vote. Mock markup is congressional custom and is not mentioned in TPA.

[71] Most staff of the other committees of jurisdiction were not involved in this process and did not offer a view.

[72] 19 U.S.C. §§ 2153, 2155.

[73] For a discussion of our selection criteria, see appendix I.

[74] TACA's charter was renewed in March 2006 after having been terminated a year and a half earlier. TACA's first meeting after its charter was renewed was in March 2007, with a second meeting in June 2007. Neither of these meetings, however, dealt with FTAs, and it held no other meetings under TPA. Furthermore, USTR officials told us that TACA members did not give advice or write an official report on any of the FTAs pursued under TPA. For these reasons, we did not include TACA in the count for our review.

[75] In response to GAO's 2002 report, GAO-02-876, the administration reorganized the trade advisory committee system in March 2004. Prior to this reorganization, the third tier committees had included 17 industry sector advisory committees and 4 industry functional advisory committees. These 21 committees were streamlined into 16 ITACs.

[76] Each governor's office designates a single contact point to disseminate and relay trade-related information between USTR and relevant state and local offices.

[77] Plenary meetings periodically bring all ATAC members or all ITAC members together in Washington, D.C., to hear presentations from cabinet-level and other high-ranking officials. The ITAC plenary meetings, for example, have been held twice a year since fiscal year 2005. The purpose of these meetings is to cover subjects of broad interest to many committees, combined with workshops on subjects of crosscutting issues.

[78] 19 U.S.C. § 2155.

[79] As TPA expired on July 1, 2007, any trade agreements that were going to fall under this legislative authority had to be signed by that date. Since the President is required to notify Congress of the intent to sign a trade agreement 90 days before doing so, this meant that the President had to

notify Congress about his intent to sign the U.S.-Korea FTA by April 1, 2007.

[80] 19 U.S.C. § 3804(f).

[81] 19 U.S.C. § 3804(f).

[82] 19 U.S.C. § 2155 (b).

[83] 19 U.S.C. § 2155 (c).

[84] After the three labor representatives temporarily resigned from ACTPN in 2000, because they felt their issues were not being addressed, the International Brotherhood of Teamsters General President joined in 2003, but resigned in 2004 citing continued disregard of advice and dissenting views, as well as failure to make the ACTPN broadly representative of labor, environment, and consumer interests. His successor was the treasurer of a local engineering union, who resigned in mid-2007. As of September 2007, the new and sole ACTPN Labor representative is the General President of the United Association of Plumbers and Pipefitters.

[85] Under 19 U.S.C. § 2155 (f), with certain exceptions, the provisions of the Federal Advisory Committee Act, 5 U.S.C. app. 2, apply to the advisory committees established under the Trade Act of 1974.

[86] 5 U.S.C. app. 2, § 6(c) (terminated by Federal Reports Elimination and Sunset Act of 1995, Pub. L. No. 104-66, § 3003, as amended).

[87] 5 U.S.C. app. 2, § 14.

[88] Miscellaneous Trade and Technical Corrections Act of 2004, Pub. L. No. 108-429, § 2004 (i)(2), 118 Stat. 2434, 2595.

[89] A Department of Labor official told us that the liaison group met twice with USTR during this 2-year period to stay abreast of trade issues.

[90] USTR and the Department of Labor restructured the LAC in May 2004, in response to our 2002 report. USTR told us that the LAC was unable to meet for 2 months after the May 2004 rechartering due to delays in getting members appointed, but letters of invitation to join the committee were not sent out until July 2004. A Department of Labor official told us that once invited, the vetting and appointment processes for new members can take over a year to complete.

Appendix I

[1] See GAO-04-233.

[2] Pub. L. No. 93-618.

[3] Pub. L. No. 92-463, 86 Stat. 770 (1972).

[4] Pub. L. No. 107-210.

[5] The second tier Trade Committee on Africa (TACA) did not hold any meetings during the time frame of TPA and did not exist for a year and a half of that period. Furthermore, USTR officials told us that TACA members did not give advice or write an official report on any of the FTAs pursued under TPA. For these reasons, we did not include TACA in the count for our review.

[6] GAO-02-876.

Appendix II

[1] Pub. L. No. 93-618, §§ 102, 151 (codified at 19 U.S.C. §§ 2112, 2191).

[2] Pub. L. No. 96-39, § 3(c).

[3] Pub. L. No. 98-573.

[4] Pub. L. No. 98-573, § 401(a).

[5] According to Hal Shapiro, the Senate Finance Committee threatened to use the gatekeeper provision to disapprove the negotiation of the U.S –Canada FTA. Furthermore, after extracting significant concessions from the President, the committee deadlocked, allowing negotiations to proceed by a thin margin. Hal Shapiro, *Fast Track: A Legal, Historical, and Political Analysis* (Ardsley, NY: Transnational Publishers, 2006), 158.

[6] Pub. L. No. 100-418, § 1103 (codified at 19 U.S.C. § 2903).

[7] Pub. L. No. 107-210, § 2104 (codified at 19 U.S.C. § 3804).

[8] Pub. L. No. 107-210, § 2107 (codified at 19 U.S.C. § 3807).

Appendix IV

[1] In this report, we compare the trade and investment relationship of the United States with countries pursued under TPA (TPA countries) to countries with which the United States neither has an FTA nor has pursued one under TPA (non-FTA countries). A third group includes those countries with which the United States already had an FTA in force prior to TPA (FTAs prior to TPA; e.g., North American Free Trade Agreement [NAFTA]).

[2] Economists point out that the imbalance between exports and imports is mirrored by the imbalance in capital flows—borrowing by the United States

(consumers, businesses, and government) outstrips U.S. investment and lending abroad.

[3] While U.S. services trade is in surplus overall for each of these groups, the value of these surpluses is relatively low in comparison to the goods trade deficits and, therefore, does not remove the overall trade deficit.

INDEX

A

B

E

F

G

H

I

J

K

L

M

S

T